Hidden to Revealed

Amber Johnson
Hidden to Revealed: A Walk With God to Find Love

—

Published by - Spines
ISBN: 979-8-89569-429-9

Hidden to Revealed

A Walk With God to Find Love

Amber Johnson

Acknowledgments

Throughout my journey, I have encountered numerous teachers, preachers, prophets, and even common folks who have poured their wisdom into my life during its most tumultuous seasons. To the Lord, I extend my deepest gratitude. I have grown to realize that it is through obedience and the unfathomable love of God that He activated His faithful servants to breathe life into my weary spirit. This mission is centered on His Kingdom, and thanks to their unwavering leadership, I am empowered to write and publish this book. Thank You, Father, and Lord Jesus, for being the ultimate solution in this existence. Thank You for transforming my identity and cleansing my wrongdoings. Thank You for selecting me and gracing me with the privilege to share Your gospel among Your beloved people. I cherish You, Papa, and my beloved Big Brother.

- Daughter Hephzibah (Amber)

Prologue

I offer a glimpse into my journey, a testament meant to encourage others to embrace the guidance of the Holy Spirit. My life has been a winding road, but God has redeemed the time I squandered. Long before I put pen to paper for this book, He whispered to me that wisdom and understanding would come swiftly, a message not meant to boast but to reveal the steadfastness of the Lord and His calling for each of us. His swift action restored what I thought was lost, an act of grace, mercy, and love that redirected me onto the narrow path leading to Him. It is my hope that within these pages, readers find the inspiration to cultivate their own relationship with God, learning to connect with Him in those quiet moments when the world falls silent. When no eyes are upon you, how do you converse with the Holy Spirit, with Jesus, and with our Father in Heaven?

In writing, I reflect on pivotal moments of my life, concluding each chapter with selected journal entries, treasured insights God has permitted me to share. These entries unveil my thoughts and feelings during various seasons. As you turn the pages, you will witness the healing that the Lord continues to work within me. To protect the privacy of those mentioned, I have adapted their names into biblical ones with a touch of whimsy. This space I've created is both vulnerable and sacred, a calling from God that I must fulfill. I pray earnestly that the Lord moves through these words to reach those grappling with similar struggles. It can be daunting to open up to others—but with God, you always have permission to be honest.

I've endeavored to keep my journal entries largely unedited to preserve their authenticity. In my conversations with the Lord, I speak as I would to a trusted friend—someone I hold dear. I reject the need for perfection in those sacred moments spent with Him. Bear with me if you encounter fragmented sentences or minor errors; it is authentic connection that the Lord values above all. Jesus does not call the qualified; He qualifies those He calls. This book, inspired by the Holy Spirit, unveils part of my journey chasing love and how I discovered true love in Him. I pray that the glorious salvation of our Lord envelops you, transforming your interior self to radiate His glory outwardly. May the God of Abraham, Isaac, and Jacob bless you abundantly; may His countenance shine upon you and bring you grace. May the Lord's gaze be upon you, granting peace as you abide in His presence all the days of your life. I ask this in the name of Christ Jesus. Amen.

Chapter 1

Overlooking God

Looking back, it's clear to me that divine intervention shaped my journey. I remember those long, quiet nights of rocking myself to sleep, consumed by desperate thoughts of ending my own existence. My unspoken sorrows echoed in the silence. Unheard tears rolled down my face with my sister beside me, both of us crammed into a full-sized bed. For countless nights throughout my childhood and adolescence, we navigated the struggles of being part of a lower-income family, always striving, always hoping, just to get by.

In my past existence, I roamed freely, spoke my mind, and lived entirely on my own terms. Unlike most children who have clear ambitions and dreams, mapping out their futures with big aspirations, I found myself adrift, lacking a defined purpose. It seemed that while my peers were busy chasing their passions—selecting colleges and eyeing careers—I was mired in indifference. Interests eluded me, and passion was a distant concept. Others branded me as lazy, painting my lack of ambition in harsh colors. I truly had no clarity about the direction I wanted to take in life. Constantly, I found myself feeling out of sync with those around me.

My mother exerted her utmost effort to bring us to church, believing in the salvation it could offer, yet the pastor's words were lost on me, failing to address the struggles I faced with mental illness. For me, religion offered no liberation, limited as it was to a narrow understanding. I had heard tales of God and His immeasurable goodness, yet my eyes were only met with the stark realities of sin, chaos, and an overwhelming agony that cloaked my existence. How can one reconcile the notion of a benevolent God with the absence of true peace in our lives? It was a paradox I wanted no part in. As a child, the guiding influence of the Holy Spirit was but a faint murmur; proper examples of faith were absent, leaving me in ignorance of the salvation that awaited. "Trust no man," I was cautioned time and again during my formative years. Ironically, this very motto proved to be their undoing, for it made me question not only strangers but also the intentions of those who raised me. The Holy Spirit, I believed, was merely a fleeting presence felt during church services—an elusive fire that flickered brightly amidst hymns, only to leave me in the cold grip of a hellish reality afterward. Outside the sanctuary, life returned to its disordered state: the haze of smoke clouded my lungs, curses flew from our lips, and commitment felt like a shackle rather than a bond. Unwavering allegiance to family was the only form of devotion that mattered, far beyond the trivialities of marriage. In my family, God was seen as a distant authority, known only through the rigidity of religion and the burden of rules. However, He is the God of connection and guidance. There existed no vibrant relationship with Him—a belief pervasive in our lives that He was uninterested in healing our wounds or conversing with us. Instead, He was viewed as a sporadic giver, bestowing blessings at random, only to turn a blind eye as we returned to our sinful ways. The suffering we endured was often self-inflicted, a product of choices made in the shadows, far from the light of divine grace.

As a young child, shadows of depression and insecurity stalked me relentlessly; I was haunted by the belief that other kids silently judged me. I was the heavier child, never acquainted with the notion of being slim or healthy, tipping the scales at nearly 200 pounds by the tender age of ten. That weight set me apart, creating an invisible barrier that forbade friendship. My kindergarten teacher's report card bore the words: "needs to work on confidence and self-esteem." Yet those words were not paired with guidance; my family's lifelong struggle with their own weight left little room for deeper conversations. The singular advice looped in my head: "just lose the weight. My insecurities set me on a relentless pursuit of love and lust, as I found no pleasure in the world surrounding me. When I hit my preteen years, a rising curiosity about sexual intimacy led me down the dark path of pornography. At that innocent age, I was oblivious to how deep the addiction would sink its claws into me, making it increasingly difficult to break free. My consumption of porn wasn't merely for the sake of sexual release; instead, my inquisitiveness drove me to wonder what a relationship might entail. Yet, with each viewing, my insecurities blossomed, magnified by the glaring realization that I looked nothing like those polished actors and actresses on the screen. By the time I turned thirteen, I found myself in my first relationship with a boy my age, albeit long-distance, and my heart ached for him. My infatuation spiraled into a dangerous affection, wherein I cherished him more than I did myself, unwittingly allowing my vulnerabilities to be exploited. We were both young and naïve, desperately seeking fulfillment in all the wrong ways. To bridge the miles, we exchanged provocative videos, hoping to ease the void that separated us. Having never experienced sexual intercourse, I was blind to the reality that the devil was stealing not just my innocence but my purity as well. The adversary will exploit **every single doubt** to rob, ruin, and obliterate the beautiful future that God has designed for you.

I surrendered my virginity while indulging my own flesh, a moment I had always yearned to offer away in a natural, timely manner. Instead, I transgressed against my own body, engulfed in waves of regret and shame as I witnessed blood—a stark reminder of my shame. The burden of having lost my virginity through my own hands weighed heavily on me, leaving me grieving for years until grace found me. Throughout my youth, I felt invisible to the opposite sex, plagued by the toxic belief that my lost purity rendered me unworthy, amplifying my anxiety. For nine tumultuous years, I navigated a long-distance relationship, a constant back-and-forth that defined my teenage and early adult life. At twenty, when we finally met face to face, I gave myself to him, both physically and emotionally. Yet, after all that longing and the allure of intimacy, I found no satisfaction. It was a relationship marred by toxicity, where he and I was emotionally distant, and I won't assign blame; each of us carried our burdens. Misery, it seemed, had become my closest companion. I longed for the comfort and truth that could have nurtured my mental health. This was my genesis—a collision of traumas that, though painful, ultimately redirected my path toward God. For this, I am grateful.

It was good for me to be afflicted so that I might learn your decrees.
The law from your mouth is more precious to me than thousands
of pieces of silver and gold.
Psalms 119:71-72 NIV

16 September 2016

So today was pretty great, may I say? The first day of Fall Conference is completed and I have thoroughly enjoyed myself. So many amazing people and fun times. It's beautiful here. It's my first time being at a camp and the mountains. Gorgeous! I also went on a swing today! It's been forever since I was last on a swing. Literally since elementary school! I was so nervous that it would break. So scared but it didn't! It was so fun. I felt like a kid again. I felt young and carefree. Earlier, my mood switched really fast. I'm not going to write details because I don't want this to ever be read and someone to get the wrong idea. I just need to say, life really sucks. Life is and will always be random chance. I spent so many years. So many. I am the only one that can vouch for myself. I spent so long looking for my love. Looking for someone to love me. Why can't I be loved? Why is it that every year nothing changes? I've never had the opportunity to like someone and they like me back and now my nightmare is coming true. Don't get me wrong. I love my sister and she is beautiful. Both of them are, but clearly there is something wrong with me if I am having no luck, right? They both have guys that like them. Why haven't that happened to me? I'm not jealous. I mean I am but I am happy that they don't have to go through the pain I am going through. It hurts to realize you really aren't worth anyone's time. I blame most of everything on my social anxiety and of course, life can never say, "Hey. Let me give you someone who will open you up and will want to know the true you. It's not fair. My dad always tells me not to love too hard and he reminds me that I do but he doesn't really help me with how not to love hard because it's all I want. I want someone to want me. Why hasn't anyone wanted me? That's why I love hard. I have so much love to give and no one wants it. No one wants my love. Why? Why does no one want my love? Why? That's all I have asked myself for. I don't know how many years, almost a decade. I remember being a kid and thinking I can't wait to have a boyfriend when I get older in school. I would see everyone else get in relationships and little did I know I would be in college (now), thinking about younger me and telling young Amber that it didn't happen. It doesn't happen. I'm not wanted. Amber, you are not wanted. I would believe the older version of me because I was insecure growing up; teased often. I knew it. I knew it. I remember thinking and hoping I would grow up hot. Didn't happen either. I became extremely depressed starting high school. I still am but freshman year brought a whole new side of me that I had no idea I had. I'm still dealing with my problems though. I just want someone that I invest all of my time in to finally notice me. I want my love to be used. I have so much to give and I give it without receiving anything and it leaves me empty. So empty. I try hard not to cry... Not here with so many people around. I want to be needed. It's not fair. I try so hard. What's wrong with me? What? Everything. Thanks. Thank you for everything and nothing at the same time @ life. I'm tired of crying. So tired. I need sleep. Good night.

20 September 2016

Can you believe 2016 is almost over? Like, the realization is hitting me. I started college. This is all still new to me. I dreamt about this time. It's finally a reality. Well, anyway, speaking of dreams, I just remembered I needed to briefly write about the one I had. So last night, or this morning, whenever it was, I dreamt that I had an infant baby. They were mine. I don't know the gender, but I think it was a girl. But that's not important. What's important is that I loved that baby. I loved that baby so much. I love that baby now, and I'm not even dreaming. Also, I was pregnant again. I loved that baby too. I'm not sure who the dad was supposed to be, but I know I knew him. I just kept hugging and holding that baby. I love them so much.

26 October 2018

Here I am. A new me. I am writing once again in this journal. Time has surely flown by. The reason I say that I'm a new me because well a lot has changed since my last entry. For one, I am back home. I've been home for almost 2 years now. I found a job; it's not the best in the world, but I like the work and I'm finally making my own money. I believe the biggest achievement right now is that I am 80 lbs lighter than my heaviest weight. I'm still struggling mentally, but I am admitting that I am in a better headspace. I'm more confident and self-loving instead of loathing. When I decided to take a break from school, I was in such a low state of mind. Happiness seemed to stray away quickly. I wasn't doing anything but getting fatter and sitting around the house eating everything that I shouldn't have been eating. No job, no school, no friends, nothing. I lost my friends during this time too. It's too long of a story, so I won't waste my ink. I was so unhappy. One day I was standing in my room doing something... I can't quite remember it. My mother was in the bathroom doing her business and I couldn't help to take a quick glance and saw her looking at me. Maybe it's just my brain but it was a look of disgust. I was always bigger than her but I knew I was turning into more of a disappointment. I felt it in my soul. I turned away quickly and felt my heart drop. I don't remember exactly when that happened, however, it was one of the things that pushed me to my ultimate decision at 5:00 a.m. on a Tuesday morning, February 5th, to be exact, of 2018 I decided there needed to be a change. I was 19 about to be 20, no job and no school so I told myself I needed to do something. KPOP (korean pop) band Got7. My favorite group was going on tour earlier this year. I had hope that I would see them because of my new job and funds lined up. Someone on Twitter mentioned getting in shape before the concert and I thought that was a great idea. I didn't want to look like a fat pig in front of my favorite seven people, so that's when I decided to lose weight. I know that's crazy considering the million other times I have went on diets. This time I told myself to exercise, no exceptions, a daring goal of 50 lbs in half a year. I could cry at the thought. I was so scared and it was so hard, especially in the beginning. My motivation? Kim Yugyeom. I made a promise to him that I would do it. I promised on Instagram. Guess what. Five months later, I had done it. Here I am 80 lbs down and still going. I'm not so hard on myself anymore. I love my body on most days now. I haven't reached exactly 80 lbs but I'm very close and know I will get there. It has been such a long learning experience. I truly am a different person. I read about other people's weight loss experiences and hear all these stories about everything changing when you lose a significant amount of weight. It's all true and I never thought it would be. Loving myself and body is so foreign to me. I'm learning how though. I'm going to California to visit my best friend in December. I can't believe it's finally happening. Real happiness is coming. I'm still sad all the time because I'm lonely. Very lonely. No love. You know, I'm trying to take one good thing at a time. I hope one day soon I can say, "I'm truly happy." Well, that's my life update. It's been crazy but not too terrible. I could still smile.

8 February 2019

Well, well, well. Happy New Year. I really had hoped to write in this journal on New Year's, but I never got around to it. My weight loss anniversary has also passed. It was the 5th. I was 91 lbs down. As long as I get to the 100 mark by the end of the month, which I will, I will consider it 100 lbs in one year. I never thought I would get to say that. It's weird because today I looked in the mirror. I haven't in so long. Right after I worked out, I looked in the mirror, and I cried. I cried hard. I cried because I didn't recognize myself. I don't know me anymore. I'm someone completely different physically. At least I cried for younger Amber. I'm so much smaller than I have ever been. Life has been so crazy, and I'm trying to take it a day at a time. Speaking of which, I have something very important to talk about because it's life-changing for me, and I don't know what to do. I need signs. Something. So there's this guy, and I'm positive he's interested in me, and I've already decided to give him my number. However, he is the brother of an old crush! That's so awkward, but that alone isn't going to deter me. I know he is a good person, so I'm not giving him up that fast. He is soft-spoken and has a pretty smile. He seems really sweet. Well, he called me "beautiful" when I was not. Now he's the only thing I can think about! I really believe he is my gift that God has given to me. Paul wasn't "The One," but he is. I wasn't going to say names but why not? The thought that someone like him would be interested in ugly me. I felt flustered at the thought. I want this to work. I need this to work. It must work. I will probably write again about him. I pray it's happy things. I want to be happy. I always say that but it feels closer than ever. Now my time really is now. This is my prime, Amber. I hope you're proud of me. I'm really doing it now! I just like to imagine the kisses and hugs and cute things. I was horny earlier. Too horny. The thought of him screwing me is so vivid. I feel like after I lost weight I'm worse. I don't know. Maybe it's because I feel attractive and I actually look good now. I have a nice body even though I want him to love me for me. I really want him to stay because he wouldn't dare let someone that looks like me go. I don't know. I have mixed feelings about it all. I just want to be loved. Kisses are so close. Patience if it all works out. Become friends first. Do things together, then fall for each other? I can do that. Please let this work out. He is all I could think about and now I am expecting far too much. Please, Amber, don't let your hopeful spirit get the best of you again and pray he doesn't have a girlfriend. I would cry for days.

10 May 2019

Quiet when I'm coming home and I'm on my own. Dear lover, soulmate, if you're out there and if we haven't already met one another, please come to me or come back to me... Is there any way of knowing if someone is made for you? I miss Timothy like crazy. It's week seven, and I still cry like a maniac. I've deleted texts and pictures. The saddest part about them being deleted is that those were my happiest moments. My happiest moments in my whole life were in those pictures and those texts. I've never felt so whole as a person. Everyone said I had a glow. I couldn't stop smiling. I finally had something—someone—to look forward to. I finally had someone who craved me and wanted to be with me. The feeling was so foreign but so nice. I love being held with locked fingers and the way he looked at me sweetly. Okay. He was truly the sweetest boyfriend. You were my everything. I'm praying God brings him back to me. My angel. My blessing. I miss you. I miss you very much. Quickly, I became very dependent on him and looked for him to give me happiness. All I needed was reassurance but I didn't come when I needed it most. I wanted to beg him to stay. I really really did. However, I learned my lesson before from doing that. Truly, he became my oxygen. I love him. I miss him. That's all I can say. My glow has disappeared and I'm back to sad and very lost eyes. I can't lose weight because I'm stressed and keep overeating. I just want love. I want and need his love. He was so good to me. It was so nice to not be alone and hurting. I don't like hurting and it feels so much worse now. Cute boys break hearts. He was so cute. So fine and still is. I can't believe he was even mine. I can't believe he thought I was beautiful. I mean he is so gorgeous. So beautiful inside and out. It's crazy. He just intimidates me and I hate living in my fantasy world now. I have my fantasies and past. I will think about the memories with him and try to relive them and those moments just to feel something. Something other than loneliness, something other than despair and worthlessness. Our first date. Oh,how quickly I fell for him. He was amazing, good-looking, kind, and watched me with adoration. The way he bit his lip that one time when we were just sitting and talking. Neither of us wanted to go. I miss it. Our second date was a movie and walking around. He reached out to hold my hand and I internally screamed because I was dying for him to touch me. He said I looked delicious and my heart skipped several beats. I miss his compliments. Our third... I can't really remember. It gets foggy. The day he made me his and I met his mom. He hated for me to pay for him but I loved it. My baby boy. I just wanted to spoil him because he spoiled me. The flowers. The poem that I can't throw away just yet. I kept thinking if I pray over it and hold it close to my heart, you will somehow come back. Come back. Our first kiss. Slow intimate but in public. Simple but had "I adore you," all in it. Timothy, I still adore you. Please don't go. I need you. You made me feel safe and loved and wanted. I really was proud of him. You were so good. I wish he would just answer me. I still think about him as if he were mine. I like to plan the things to talk about and conversation. Things I would do to him or let him do to me. Even though I know it won't happen. The thought gives me hope. Hope is the thing that breaks my heart the most. False hope is evil. So evil.

Please come back to me. I'm willing to work with you. I know you're busy and need to focus on school and work. Make me your second priority please. Yourself comes first. I want him the most. I need him. God blessed me with him and the devil is trying to take him away. My boy. My man. I hate not being with him. I'm constantly looking for male attention but all I want is his. I miss him. I love him. I do. I love Timothy. I hate that all these people are in relationships and marrying their loved ones or having kids and I'm just here. I want to be in school with a boyfriend and a job. I want to be the person the others look at in envy. I've had to do that for years. I want to be the obnoxiously affectionate couple that hold hands and kiss in public. Love me Timothy, please. My pen is running out of ink. I wanted him to love me. I want him to choose me as his first everything. I want to be his everything. Keep thinking about me. Don't move on. Please. I'm yours. I will always be yours. I adore you. Don't move on from me please. I don't really have much else to say, to be honest. I just wanted to write about how much I miss him and how I wish he would just try once more one more time. I love you. God, please please give him back to me. My angel, my man. My soulmate, my blessing that I am forever grateful for. I waited for a text from him every day and night. No matter how much I cry, nothing seems to change. Why? I'm back to my old ways. I just don't want to be sad anymore. I don't want, in the middle of smiling or laughing, to look away and zone out at a thought of him and my eyes immediately drop with my heart. I deserve his love and I deserve him.

5 August 2019

Next weekend I get to see my baby boy. Lord protect me on my way there and during. Keep me in your hands. I know I'm irresponsible for doing things I shouldn't be. I am so excited though. 2019 really is my new beginning after 2018. I pray we stick together this time. I want us to work this time. You are the only one who knows his intentions. I pray that whatever they are, he wants to love me unconditionally. I don't want to feel fat and ugly. I'm scared. I love him. I try to tell myself that it is possible for skinny guys to like bigger girls. I miss my boy. I'm so insecure when he isn't talking to me. I said no more long distance, but here I am. I feel completely in love with my first love again. My first heartbreak.

Please let this be the thing that we were meant to be. I love you, Paul. I have got to tell him. I plan to tell him when I see him. Why is it that I have the biggest fear of being ridiculed for my body. He has basically seen all of me, even when I was extremely fat. He was the first to call me sexy. Why do I feel so big? Please love me, give me compliments. His kisses and touches will probably hush my thoughts. Seven years later and I am still someone he wants in his life. There are other things on my mind but I am so young. I shouldn't be thinking about already starting a family or marriage. All these people are doing just those things though. I want to as well. Maybe my last relationship had multiple lessons. Enjoy the moment. I'm still young. Don't look ahead. I will look ahead but not too far ahead because if heartbreak comes, it will hurt less. I'm sure after this time if it doesn't work out there will be no other time. This really is it. I love you, Paul. Please love me. Please. The thought alone of being unloved makes me tear up. I'm proud of him and want to be a part of his support system. There is no way we could just be friends. It's why I questioned him to begin with. I need to know that I have all of him. I want him only. Please want me.

11 August 2019

My stomach hurts. It's turning with anxiety and uneasiness. I'm scared. I'm so scared. I remember why I said I'd never go back to him. I remember why I said no more long distance. It wasn't just because of my anxiety and insecurity. Reassurance is unheard of with him. He barely opens up to me and he always keeps me secret. I want to see him this weekend, but I'm so scared. I know this isn't going to work out if he wants to keep me a secret. There is no reason to. He's cheating or wants to keep his chances high with others and I'm so scared to confront him but it's my heart. I hate this. I hate this. I'll know for sure after this weekend.

8 September 2019

Well, well, well. I am a changed woman since a month ago. It's been crazy. Too crazy. I don't even know where to begin. Well, let's start with my birthday weekend. When I got to the hotel, I had to wait for an hour until I seen him. He was so cute. I always call him cute. I miss him already if I'm honest, but hear me out. Anyways, I enjoyed my time with him. I did. I made a horrible mistake though. I had unprotected sex. He bought a Plan B and I'm on birth control, but that was still a No-No. He was fun and silly and we did "it" like 4 times while together. I have never been so close to someone before. It was so weird though.... Both of my boyfriends this year have had very intense features. The way they look, facial-wise is almost scary to me. Intimidating. It was hard to make eye contact. It's hard to make eye contact with people that I find good-looking. The way he watched me, had the hair on my back stand up. Felt great. The first time we did "it" was while watching Black Panther. He was so slow at first and I want him again. I don't know. I'm so confused. After the first time, he went out and got the pill and I showered then later we watched a funny movie. I just liked laying around with him. Basically, after I came back home, the following two weeks were hell! Ended up getting a UTI, had a fishy smell, and my menstruation started. On top of that, my birth control made my period light so I was worried I was pregnant and with an STI. He stop talking with me, becoming awfully quiet. He still bought me a gift for my birthday though. I was so scared that he gave me something and impregnated me, while leaving me all on my own. With anxiety and depression it was absolute hell. I had the worst time of my life. Eventually, I decided to break up with him but didn't do it until like a week later. As of now, was four days ago. He seemed to have not cared, but maybe because he was still on his break and busy. We talked today, though. He said sorry and I'm back with him... I shouldn't have. I was so proud of leaving him. I love him so much though. I want us to work badly. So badly. I adore him. I want him. He said he wants me but if anything happens like that again I will seriously drop him. I feel even worse because I spent all this time praying that if I got out of this turmoil, I would seriously be done with him. But I'm a disgrace. Is God disappointed in me? Maybe so. I've prayed for change. I want him to change for me. I know I can't make a man out of a boy. Only he can do for himself. I want to be his when he changes. If I'm really what he wants, can he please act like it and change for me? I love him. Back and forth for seven years. That's a lot of time. I want him so badly. I want him completely. If I could marry him I would. I want to move in with him, marry him, and have his children. I think we'd have cute kids. I love him. I want him. God, I'm so sorry. I'm so sorry. I'm stupid. So foolish. God, I'm praying to you to keep me safe and for him to act right.

1 November 2019

Why is it that you have no problem going all day without talking to me but I feel like dying then I try to do the same out of stubbornness? Then I realize I shouldn't have to do this with my own boyfriend. I shouldn't feel bad about asking my boyfriend to talk to me. I'm afraid I'll be ridiculed by him. I'm afraid of being ridiculed by everyone else. No one takes mental illness seriously or they all think you're crazy and run away. I don't want him to run away. I'm trying to keep him in my life this time, but I feel like we're on completely different levels. We don't talk enough for this to work in the long run but I'm trying. It's all I have right now. Am I worth the fight? Oh, how I wish I could stop crying over boys. I really wish they were the ones crying over me. That'll never happen. Well it has. It didn't feel good. Searching for happiness is so hard. Yes, I know I should be looking for it inside but I need help. I know it's possible with someone aiding me. I know if I had any relationship like earlier this year, I'd love myself sooner than without. I miss feeling loved. I don't feel loved at all if I'm honest. I don't feel as wanted as he says he wants me. Maybe that's just him. I'm trying to give the benefit of the doubt. Feels like I'm making excuses for him though, right? I'm making excuses for him to give me less than what I need. He'll consider me clingy. Maybe I don't need him. I don't know. I'm so confused. I hurt often but it might actually be due to my depression and anxiety. I love this man. I want us to work. I push to be loyal daily. Faithful. I love him. I get feelings of hurt. Pain. I love him. I'm giving him the world while mine is falling apart. Somehow I feel like he'd say, "No one told you to." Maybe he wouldn't. I want him to make time for me. I wish we were closer. I love him. Why doesn't he feel the same? Why do I feel unwanted? Well, "wanted" sexually, but not emotionally. I should be used to it. I'm almost never attached emotionally to people. I beg to change every day. Even after all this time.

Chapter 2

Chains Of Witchcraft

During this period of my life, I unexpectedly found solace in the world of new-age witchcraft. The allure of psychic readings, astrology, tarot, and the mysteries of zodiac signs captivated my imagination. I had never delved into the Bible nor acquainted myself with Christ Jesus. Yet, I found myself engaging in conversations with God the Father, while others chose to label Him as the "universe." Though I could not distinctly hear His voice, fleeting signs and signals seemed to guide my way. In my naïveté, I dabbled in witchcraft and divination, unwittingly surrendering myself to the enemy and granting him dominion over my spirit. For years, confusion and chaos penned the chapters of my life, stretching from 2020 to 2023. As the end of my long-distance relationship loomed, I transformed my bedroom closet into a sacred prayer space. Within those four walls, I felt safe to voice my deepest fears to God. I approached Him with raw vulnerability, burdened by the weight of my sorrows. At that moment, salvation felt worlds away, and I navigated a tumultuous sea of uncertainty, ignorant of the path to redemption. I poured out my heart, confessing the pain the relationship had inflicted upon me, weary of shedding tears daily for two long years. Despite writing down the qualities I desired in a husband, God would gently remind me that my former partner was not meant for me.

In the fog of my emotions, I fought against His words, crying out in anguish and admitting my lack of understanding of Jesus' role in cultivating my relationship with Him. I mistakenly believed that my closeness with the Father was enough and that our chats made Him a friend of comfort. But in truth, I was still distant, and my connection was only possible through the Son. Each time I emerged from my prayer closet, heavy tears streaming down my face, I sensed His disappointment with my return to what had caused my pain. A few years later, the profound truth struck me: He had to let me wander back into the shadows, as I had yet to embrace salvation or surrender my life to Christ. In those moments, I felt no binding duty to heed His guidance. Bound by the lies of the enemy —twin flames, past lives, and distorted doctrines—I remained trapped in a toxic cycle that threatened my very essence. The enemy excels at weaving counterfeit relationships and situations to distract us from the divinely ordained path.

In the year 2021, everything shifted. I emerged as an unexpected risk-taker following my weight loss journey. I began to awaken from the fog of that unhealthy relationship. I found myself discontent in both my job and my relationship. In a frantic search for happiness, I turned my gaze outward, hoping to find something to spark joy within me. On a fateful day I ventured into my new delivery gig, I crossed paths with my Godsent future husband. There was no immediate attraction, yet, in retrospect, it seemed to carry a weight of meaning. In that moment, I had no inkling of his true identity, yet deep within me stirred the recognition that only God could unveil him at a time when I wasn't even searching. The first day of my delivery gig unfolded brilliantly, and with exhilaration coursing through me, I took a leap of faith to quit my stable, albeit painful, job. It felt liberating to break free from that cocoon of physical discomfort and strive towards disentangling myself from the toxic relationship that had long held me captive. It was then that, in the divine orchestration of the universe, God illuminated a path for me to follow.

"The path of the righteous is like the morning sun, shining ever brighter till the full light of day."
Proverbs 4:18 NIV

1 January 2020

Here's to the new year. Here's to new beginnings. Here's to new trials and errors. This year it will be very emotional. I think this would have been the year I graduated if I had stayed in school so it will hurt a bit. I'm rooting for everyone though. It will be my year also. I'm starting my second weight loss journey this year. I will get to my goal. I'm going into the new year with a clear mind and goals with the love of my life. We still have ups and downs but I believe we will get there. I started watching tarot readings again. They are giving me some kind of hope. I'm headed toward commitment and marriage. I can only hope, that it's true. I can only hope. The reason that we are still together is because of the one-word "soulmates," and the thought that God is keeping us together this time. It has given me lots of hope. I want to be with him. I want him to be with me. My anxiety will not ruin me this year. I can't wait to see him. He tells me the same. I adore him. I'm trying to give him space when he needs it. Somehow I feel that it's working. It's driving me crazy, but if it just means I have to be less clingy, then I will go through it. If it's meant to be then it will be. I wish I could have kissed him last night. Maybe one year? I'm trying to hold on to that hope. You're so cute. I'm a creeper. As you know, I found the cutest picture online with his smile. I'm in love. I love his smile. I truly believe God gave me the ability to fall in love hard. However, if there is a such thing as soulmates, maybe I was just naturally attracted to him for solely that purpose. When I look back, I'm like how? LOL. But fate truly. My life line has him in it. Maybe even to bare his children also, God willing. It's just so weird. I don't know what makes me want him so badly. I don't know what makes me fall in love. I just do. I admit I may not know him as much as I should. I'm trying to learn him though. I will learn him. This year will be different. I know I have many hopes to improve my mental and physical state. I will be better all around this time next year. I claim it. That's really everything I wanted to say, I think. I'll write next time,if not. Happy 2020, Amber. Let's do it right this time.

12 January 2020

You're probably wondering why I'm writing so early in the morning. I'm wondering the same. I was filled with emotions this morning. Sadness. Regret for many situations I had no control over because they were my consequences. I'm still so broken and holding on to younger me. I can't let her go because she was so alone and all she had was me, as a child. I ate. I ate so much. I just never understood why there were other big girls that got into relationships, except me. What made me so different? My anxiety and depressive personality probably. I know life isn't fair. I know. But after all those nights crying and crying, hoping to find someone while growing up, just wasn't enough. I was given long distance, A tease. It only makes me feel worse. I'm only good enough for a long-distance relationship. I can't have the real thing. No one realizes how hard it was for me. So anyways, the reason why I'm talking about this is because anytime I see a picture of my love with another girl from prom or wherever, even if it was years ago, I still get incredibly jealous and insecure. It's like, I know he would have had other girlfriends like everyone else. Why couldn't I have the same? I didn't go to prom or dance because if I would have went alone, the pain of seeing other couples would have ruined me. I wanted to be taken so badly. Not one person. No matter how much I fantasized about being asked, would actually go with me. Then I think about how it should have been me and him but because we were long-distance it would have never happened. The younger me still lives inside. I don't want to leave her but she's causing me so much pain. I want to be loved now. Thank you. I always wanted to be. I don't want long-distance anymore. I've been through it already. Like why do I still have to deal with it? I want to be loved whole. My heart is almost already weak. My brain is a mess. I just want to be important. The other day I forgot to write about it but there was a sketchy post written to Paul and I immediately asked him who that woman was. I was ready to argue. I needed an explanation. I can't sit here and waste my time. Which I still feel like it may happen. He called me immediately and we talked about it. He cleared it up and we were good again. I don't want my anxiety to ruin anything. I want us to work out. The little girl inside of me just won't quiet her thoughts. He's handling my temper well this time. I'm scared I'm feeding into lies. It's not that I don't trust him... Well, I don't know. It's my thoughts that make me feel that way. He is a terrible texter but when he talks to me I feel loved and wanted. Same when we're together. I love him. I do. Now that we've started visiting each other, I feel so much better. The tarot card readings have given me so much hope for better things. I want commitment. We've been together for almost seven months now. We still have some ways before a year, but I can't wait. I keep thinking about if we're going to ever move in with one another? That day will be the best day of my life probably. I will finally have him in my arms daily. I will miss him but he will come back home to me. Laying next to him waking up in the middle of the night to watch his pretty eyes as he sleeps. I remember praying for the long term. I remember praying that this time would be it. As he slept and I watched. I nearly cried. I pray this is only the beginning of where our love truly is. I don't want to compare us to anyone else. This is our story. I'm done writing. I've had too many different emotions in this entry. I'm tired and still have to get up to work out. Hope to write soon.

7 May 2020

I'm so in love with him and it feels like he doesn't feel anything towards me. I swear I love this man. Somehow he came to me. If it's not meant to be, then this is the longest lesson and punishment ever. I love him. I do. When I'm upset I feel dizzy and sick. It's nothing new, but sometimes it feels stronger? I only say this because it's how I feel right now. Dizzy. Kind of shaky. I miss him. He doesn't talk to me. I'm not important to him. I'm so unhappy. I'm not supposed to be this unhappy but I want him. It makes me sad because looking at other people, they're happy. I want that. I want to be happy. I miss being happy and trying to hang on because maybe he wants me. I wanted to be his best friend and lover. Don't communication comes with that? Talking to their loves. I don't talk to mine. I want to be his support system but he can't be that for me. This isn't how it's supposed to be. Why am I holding on? I need reassurance. I'm annoying now though. I can't ghost him again. I don't want to. I can't break up with him. I have to waste another year, don't I? If nothing changes then I will go after a year. Things should be different, right? I need to be loved and craved. I need someone to want me to themselves. I want someone to cherish and appreciate my efforts and love. I need someone to make me a priority, just as I do them. I should be the first, where they run to express their emotions. I want to be their best friend. If I'm significant, why am I treated like last? Why can't I get basic 'significant other' attention and affections? I hate this. I hate life. Why can't I be loved? Why can't I be happy? Why can't I have the proper love and affection? I miss being happy. I miss feeling above the clouds. Just feeling as if I was in heaven. I miss finally thinking that this life wasn't or isn't hell. That things like this would exist in hell. But this. Oh, this would. I miss feeling happy. I'm sad. I'm so sad. I should be somewhere smiling with arms cradling me. I should be somewhere feeling beautiful and absolutely in love with reciprocated actions. What happened to that? I miss that. I miss the heart fluttering feeling. I miss being so happy that I didn't want to end myself. For the first time and so long I had completely forgot what it was like to be suicidal for an entire month. I was able to feel complete bliss, then all at once I was hit by a train. Going 80 to 90 miles per hour. I don't know what happened that day, but I think it changed me. I was filled with something that I had prayed would stay away. Pain still lingers. My heart is still weak and probably always will be. I screamed and cried. No one knew how happy I was then than in my entire life. I was so weak after crying everyday for months. Heavy crying. It was so hard. I survived but I'm still hurting. I think I jumped into a relationship with Paul too fast. He was so consistent in the beginning, hooking me immediately only for it all to change suddenly. Everything changed. I just want to feel important. I know he's busy, but when is he going to tell his friends at least once that he needs to be with me or do something with me? Reassure me? I don't know anymore. I'm tired of crying and wishing things could be different even after I've talked about my needs. I'm tired. Nothing is happening.

23 August 2020

I don't really have too much to say other than I'm starting my new job Monday. Tomorrow. I'm excited and nervous for this new life. Night shift is going to be hell. I'm ready for whatever I need to do. That other job was just not sustainable. I need money. I need a place of my own. I need to move on. I feel so stuck in every aspect of my life. I need change. I hate always writing about Paul, but I'm always praying for more with him. I don't understand the crap he does. I understand he's busy but he forgot my birthday and made no promise to make it up. Why do I tolerate this? I argued with him for 2 days and I don't think anything will change. It's so hard to keep holding on to him though because I'm not happy. I'm not happy at all. I cried so much on my own birthday night and more. He won't do anything different and I'm getting tired.

29 August 2020

First week at my new job is done. I actually really like it. Night shift is actually so good. It makes days go by fast and the fact that I only work 4 days is wonderful. I can't wait to see what my check will look like. They had me standing and watching for 3 days straight and my legs were so sore. I finally started working Thursday night. My legs didn't hurt as much. On top of that, my period started the day of my first day. I'm still learning of course, but the job is easy, sometimes confusing. I'll get it though. I like working with people that work just as hard or can help you. We even took a two and a half hour break Thursday night/Friday morning. It was wonderful, especially that nap. It's so hard to get on a good eating schedule. I'm trying to fit in the perfect time to work out but so far I've only done it like twice this week. I've been gaining rapidly, could be water but I've been eating crappy so I'm not so sure. I like my co-workers too. It's not a bad atmosphere to be in. That's all the good stuff before I get into my normal. I have no idea what's going on. I felt like a terrible girlfriend earlier. I'm tired of being unhappy. When he calls me to talk about the issues, he calms me so much. It's like falling back in love again. I love him and I was so close to ending it again. I don't try to use our time to talk out problems but it's been happening and nothing changes. I love him so much. He is my everything. I don't know what it is. I just do. I hate arguing with him. We've been together or known each other for so long. 8 years. After 8 years, we still choose each other. He's so good to me when we're together. I just hate the time apart. Oh, if I could see him every weekend I would. I love him. I love him. I love him. The distance kills me right. Maybe we are doing a karmic relationship thing. What if in a past life there was no distance but something happened that forced this life? Like I've said before, I think I've had many kids in another life. The line under my belly button. Small things pregnant women go through, I've been going through since I was so young. I now have mom body. I don't know. It's just weird. I literally have the body of a mother. I couldn't have a normal body after losing 120 lb. Paul has been with me since the beginning, when I was so big. I was so insecure. I never knew what made him come to me and there were so many other girls. He made me feel good being called sexy. Am I wrong for being with him? I have that attachment? He wasn't the only person to love me when I was bigger but he stayed the longest and maybe I have that attachment. My first love. I broke my hymen at the thought of him. I was like 14. He still remembers. I gave my virginity to him twice. I have that attachment. I just remember being in the middle school, wishing he went to the same school as me. I dreamt of the days we'd be together. I kept thinking he wouldn't want me if he saw me in person. Last year when we met up, it was surreal. My lifetime partner. My childhood lover. We were on and off but most of that was my issues. I'll never forget when I was in college and he wanted to visit me in Myrtle Beach. I couldn't. I was fat. I couldn't because I was deathly afraid of having sex. The idea of being naked in front of him was traumatic alone. Now it's just our time. I want to make our relationship strong. I want to be unbreakable. I love him. I want to be with him always to make up for all the time we didn't have together. I can't wait until we live together! I literally want to have his babies. That's what I actually want. I want an entire family. I don't know what has me so attached to him. I literally want his children. I have no idea what makes me crave it so much. The idea of giving him his first baby making him a father. Gives my stomach butterflies at the idea of mothering his children. I don't want to be a baby mama, though. I want to be married with a happy pregnancy. I don't know. I still remember my baby dream, all those years ago. I love that baby so much, so much. The love was so strong now so many people are having their own and it kind of makes me want some. I'm not sure but I think he wants me to have his kids too. Anyways, I don't know if it was his way of dirty talk or I don't know. I love him though. I want a baby. I'm not ready for one though. Anyways, let me go to sleep. I'm tired obviously.

26 September 2021

I thought I could write but it hurts again. So, here I am Amber. Please don't go back. There are so many good things ahead of you. I see you happy. I can see you finally getting what you deserve. The life you deserve with no excuses. You aren't crying everyday and you're finally doing it. 'It' you might ask? Loving yourself for someone whole to love you back. I know it's going to be hard for a while. The dream. The dream you had. Your story is better than the rest. We will still win and be happy.

19 October 2021

It's late so I can't take too long to write. I have to work tonight. I haven't told and written about my life unfortunately. From my spiritual awakening and journey to ending my long-term relationship and now, quitting my job. Yeah, it's been extremely hectic. I don't know why I chose now to write about it but I will say the gist of it all. My spiritual journey has been going well. I should say I'm highly aware that I'm being guided. My intuition has heightened. My guides and God loves me so much. I finally know that I am loved and protected even. I finally listened to them and got out of my relationship last month. I don't really want to talk about it much, but I'm sure I won't forget. He had much bigger plans than just being busy, even if I don't know the whole story. I hope he gets help. He'll find something better for him, as I will do the same for me. I'm healing and forgiving myself for putting up with the worst behavior. I don't hate him. Truly, will love him forever but from a distance. My twin flame. Thank you for pushing me to my awakening. I'm grateful for you and the way you treated me. I understand. I'm also so sorry to God and my guides. They were yelling at me and my mind was like "No I have to push through." I learned boundaries. They gave me my 'tower moment.' The final one. I know he probably loved me and didn't know how to show it. That's what I hope.

In other news, the guy I met at the beach was a NOPE, as well. He texted me saying that he was kicked out. I'm so sorry to hear that, but you can't stay with me! Haha. I had to laugh at the audacity to ask me. I haven't talked to him since. I hope he's okay though. He didn't have a car either. Not relationship material at all. So that's gone. I'm single. I did ask if Aaron wanted to try again. You know as I write that, it sounds like I'm just trying to find someone. I am not looking for a rebound but someone who will actually love me. I want to gain trust, friendship, and love. I was thinking about it earlier; about how I crave affection. I didn't have much growing up and I craved it badly. It's sad how much I wanted to be touched but when I finally was, I reeled. It's getting dark, so I can't rant too much but the last thing to mention is my job. Yes, I was guided from my heart to quit and do food delivery. I know it's temporary but I feel many opportunities opening for me. I love my guides and God because I know they're forcing me to do this LOL. Not like "forcing" but we have such a good relationship that they really don't want me to start doubting myself. I feel it now. Things are going to be okay. I know it's going to be okay. I have two weeks left at my job and my new life will begin. Here's to the new world and new mind. I love you

Chapter 3

Adultery, Break-Ups, And Meds

After an exhausting stretch of feeling adrift, tirelessly scouring the job listings to cover the bills, and grappling with the relentless weight that seemed to settle on my body after embarking on that graveyard shift, I found myself crashing once more into the depths of despair. In the two years following the aftermath of my shattering eight-year relationship, I stumbled through a few fleeting connections, each one leaving an imprint on my heart. Among these encounters was a married man I met at work, who unwittingly reawakened my latent childhood wounds. The attention he lavished upon me, like sweet nectar, momentarily filled the void left by my deep-seated need for affirmation. His flattery, the compliments that flowed like honey, and his generous acts of service ensnared me into a whirlwind of confusion and desire. In my desperation, I found myself praying—a heartbreaking act—calling out to God for another woman's husband. Just writing that admission twists the knife of regret deeper into my chest. I carried the burden of being labeled a "homewrecker," a moniker that haunted me as I justified my choices. In my skewed worldview, I believed I was justified in my actions, thinking he was simply unhappy in his marriage. Yet, deep down, I was tragically mistaken. The solitary time we crossed the boundaries of friendship, engaging physically, something shifted. A conviction gripped him that I could not grasp; it struck him first, long before I felt its prickling sting. I ruminated over why we couldn't forge something lasting together, interpreting it as another personal rejection, oblivious to the profound nature of his growing consciousness. Although we decided to end our chaotic affair, the air between us was transformed rather than awkwardly laden with silence. Remarkably, we remained friends, and in an unexpected twist, God would later use him to guide me toward a new season of growth.

Fast forward to the present; I find myself navigating the path of celibacy and abstinence, now stretching over a year and a half. The weight of my last relationship, one that nearly shattered my spirit, still lingers vividly in my mind. Despite the allure of his sweet words and striking demeanor—a magnetic presence that captivated me both in and out of the bedroom—he was unlike anyone I had known before. But as the days turned into weeks, he chose to ghost me, leaving me floundering in a sea of confusion and frustration. This sudden absence pushed me to act in ways I had never imagined; I caught myself standing outside his house, knocking fervently on a door that felt as though it held my sanity at bay. In that moment of reckless desperation, I paused, the question resonating painfully in my mind: "What am I doing?" February became a sorrowful month of mourning—a time when tears fell freely, and self-doubt plagued my thoughts. I questioned my worth and yearned for the belief that someone might love me with a heart overflowing with genuine affection. But as the calendar flipped to March 2023, something shifted. I decided to prioritize my mental health earnestly, seeking help from an online medication company that had first captured my attention through an ad on the television in my ex's home. It was there I confronted the harsh realities of my long-standing battles with depression and anxiety. After years spent wrestling with pride and evading counseling, I finally accepted the prescriptions that would begin to untangle the knots of my psyche. In a turbulent whirlwind, heaven and hell seemed to collide, setting me on a path toward healing that felt both daunting and interwoven with glimmers of hope.

> When Jesus saw him lying there, and knew that he already had been in that condition a long time, He said to him, “Do you want to be made well?” The sick man answered Him, “Sir, I have no man to put me into the pool when the water is stirred up; but while I am coming, another steps down before me.” Jesus said to him, “Rise, take up your bed and walk.” And immediately the man was made well, took up his bed, and walked. And that day was the Sabbath.
> *John 5:6-9 NKJV*

14 March 2023

I was practically yelling at myself to write "Amber. Write!" It's been like 2 years. How do I even do this anymore? Hahaha, much to talk about but not enough time to write all about it. My handwriting isn't as good as it once was either. What do I talk about? This is my chance to spill all the tea. Life has been so weird and wild. Last year I was quitting jobs left and right. I was looking for something that I could be happy doing for a few years. Coming up on 6 months, I've been with my current company as a warehouse associate. I love the company. Technically, I've been with them since my last entry as a food delivery driver. I went through numerous different jobs, even a work-from-home job, and hated it. I'm feeling okay now with my place of business. I'm not with Paul and haven't been with him for a while. I've had a few new people since, but no luck. My last relationship really threw me for a loop. I've got to write about it. I'm still healing and that's one of the reasons I've been dying to write. Mark... High School... I've known him since then. He lied to me. I won't write like he was the best thing to ever happen to me. I will write what he did and how he made me feel. I deserve to be honest with myself. I deserve to talk about the pain they caused me, without worrying about me being 'mean.' Mark was a liar. He lied to me. He said I was a high school crush and all.

He said he would communicate with me and all. He talked so nicely to me and ALL. He made love to me and all... He ghosted me. He went to another girl, an ex of his, I'm sure of it. "You will see your answer in a dream." I saw it in a dream and sure enough, it hurt. I don't think I'll talk about it in depth because it's not something I want to remember. Even though I know I will. I will remember this betrayal. It hurt me so much. I feel like I shouldn't trust anyone. I shouldn't. It only lasted for a month. I'll move on. I'd be lying to myself if I didn't acknowledge the fact that I still crave his attention and validation and touch. He was so good. So nasty. So good. I don't want to think about him. He still makes me sad. I know not to beg for another man to love me. Go back to your ex since you are still learning that. I hope she chooses herself too. A 'sorry' man will always be sorry. In better news, I'm on meds years later. I'm finally getting help through medicine. Is it working? I don't know. It could be better but I'm only on my third week and I'm upping my dosage soon. That's all I had to say. I hope it doesn't take me another 2 years until I write again. Time flies quickly. So many changes and not enough time. I pray the next time I write I'm in a happy successful relationship. Thank you, God.

31 March 2023

It's no accident. Nothing is an accident. I miss writing. I miss letting my feelings out on paper for God, angels, and the universe to hear me. Hear me loud and pray for courage to one day admit how broken I actually was. It's about to be April already. Time is flying. I have so much to talk about. Where to begin? My hand cramps up now when I write. It's so hard for me. I'll just start with what's on my chest right now. A guy from work. He's covering while my manager is away. I like him though. I admitted it to him. He's so cool and funny and nice to talk to. Somewhere inside of me, I want him to like me too. Tonight I'm in a wave of anxiety about texting him. I wouldn't normally go after him. I don't think I want him to make the first move, but he wouldn't. Maybe. The first few minutes of talking to him I thought I was going to like him. He has such a likable personality. My coworker said she had a crush on him too. I think she is trying to turn me away from him somehow. I'm also probably overthinking it. I'm nervous. It'll be weird but I might wait until after the week. He's handsome, kind, a good speaker, smart, and has some money! ;) Haha. When we talk, we're getting to know each other. I could listen to him speak for a long time. We bonded over The Legend of Zelda video games, my music playlist, our ADHD minds, and old jobs. I'm sitting here smiling as I write. Wow, I think I'm in this too deep already. I guess I'm writing really for peace to calm my nerves and heart. That was weird. It was almost instinct. I'm being protected. I'm watched over. I was about to say bring me peace, if this is a guy I should pursue. My heart calmed almost immediately. I know I'm protected. God and the angels are watching over me from the past and all my demons. I dreamt it. Demons, with yellow eyes, charged full sprints at me. Only to slam into an invisible wall like a ragdoll, to the ground. I think they're telling me that I'm ready. I'm so sleepy now. Whoa, how I love God so much. I love my guardian angels so much too. I must have an amazing batch. Please continue to watch over me. Guide me. I only want to follow you. I'm going to go to sleep now. Bye.

3 April 2023

The cycle is closing. My wheel of Fortune is turning. It feels like the devil won today. God always has the last laugh. I did it today. I reached out to a guy that isn't normally my type. It seems good. He seems too good for me... the old me and insecure me. I want to go after what I deserve. I don't deserve half love but full love. All effort and loyalty. I deserve it all. Today was hard. The devil did all he could to break me. God please protect me tonight, tomorrow and always God. I hope you understand. I didn't want to beg this time. I want it bad but I didn't want to cling on. I deserve him. I deserve someone who will give me all of themselves. I don't want the past. The past was so much pain. I can't go back. New love and light is what I'm chasing after. I know I'm not supposed to see my future. I'm not supposed to know the outcome. I don't want to know. I want to find love and joy. He made me so excited for work and all. I wanted to be someone to him, please. Begging feels so wrong. That's what went down the last time. I got what I wanted but it was stripped away from me. I don't want that again. With all my lessons, I should know not to hold on too tight. I really wanted to be someone to him. God, I pray I didn't embarrass myself. God, I pray for protection not only with me but with him as well. The devil would attack his mind as well if we were meant to be. I pray for love, peace, effort, and time to grow between us. I pray for your joy and guidance for a long-term happy relationship, marriage, family, and happiness in your precious name. Amen.

Chapter 4

God Or Hallucinations?

Within a few days of my prescription, I found myself stepping back into the realm of 'normalcy' for most, yet unfamiliar ground to me. Happiness coursed through me, my smile vibrant and rooted in a genuine part of my soul, a reflection of light breaking through the clouds of doubt. I was able to engage in conversations without the haunting grip of anxiety shackling my thoughts, feeling free as if my voice was a bird finally released from its cage. But as the month rolled on, something inexplicable began to stir within my nights. I would wake to the sound of my own voice, reaching out into the stillness, only to find myself startled awake by my fervent outbursts. It became routine, this dance of sleep and waking, a strange blend of reality and ethereal. In these deep slumbers, I encountered not just dreams, but ghostly visitors. Some nights, I would awake, sensing the weight of presence above me—figures, spirits, or shadowy silhouettes looming at the edge of my consciousness, whispering secrets into my ear, their words lost like whispers in the wind. One particularly vivid night, a sharp double-tap on my leg interrupted my dreams, initially dismissed as an unsettling muscle twitch. But the sensation came again, and a mix of annoyance and confusion washed over me as I momentarily believed it was one of my sisters, playfully rousing me from my deep slumber, despite their absence from my home. With a quick movement, I rose to confront the disturbance, only to be met by the striking image of a young lady draped in a dark silhouette, her hair meticulously wrapped. She stood before me, arms confidently crossed, as though she was poised and waiting for my awakening. Just as abruptly as she appeared, she dissipated into the night. Sharing this experience with my younger sister unveiled a haunting truth: our father's cousin met her end long ago within the very walls of our home, her spirit perhaps lingering still. We speculated that maybe she was a protective presence, possibly concerned about my restless sleeping habits. My father often spoke of an unseen guardian, a deathly figure that roamed our family lineage. Perhaps this apparition was simply safeguarding me, watching over my subconscious as I drifted between realms.

Amidst these spectral visitations, vivid dreams unfolded like intricate tapestries. In one unsettling reverie, I found myself outside, haunted by an invisible entity stalking me on all fours. I could trace its chaotic movements through the soft imprints it left on the grass, tangible proof of its unyielding pursuit. Just when despair threatened to consume me, a radiant white figure burst forth, heroically battling the demon that sought to ensnare me. Another dream enveloped me in a different kind of terror. I stood on my father's porch, staring down the road, when I noticed malevolent figures materializing in the driveway by the mailbox. These were no ordinary shadows but evil entities, summoned forth with supernatural speed, racing towards the sanctuary of my home. As they collided with an unseen barrier encasing our dwelling, they were repelled, tumbling helplessly onto the porch. Their determination was palpable, an insatiable hunger for entry. I remained oblivious to their true purpose until the last two or three figures advanced closer. The final demon, desperate and frantic, nearly breached our defenses, prompting me to leap from my sleep, heart racing, convinced that it had broken through, eager to reach me.

Another dream haunted my nights: I found myself in a dimly lit void, locked in a battle of wills with Death himself, a dull figure with hollow eyes who mercilessly stabbed me in the stomach with a blade forged from despair. Gasping for air as life ebbed away, he leaned closer and sneered, "Why won't you die?" I didn't answer him, for my resolve was profound—my heart pulsed with the thought, "Because I have God on my side." Silence enveloped us like a suffocating shroud, his knife piercing my flesh two more agonizing times before he hissed menacingly, "I will be back." Just then, everything faded to black, and I was jolted awake, heart racing in the shadows of my room. Two or three nights later, an ominous pattern emerged. Awakened at exactly 4:40 am, I was met with thunderous knocks reverberating through the stillness of my father's home. Panic clawed at me; surely, someone was attempting to break in! Yet, if they were truly intent on invasion, why beat against the door like a storm? They could effortlessly demolish the barrier and seize whatever attracted their malicious gaze. I pinched my skin repeatedly, fear pulsing through me—a desperate plea for reassurance that this was not another delirious hallucination brought on by the vengeful grip of my mind. As I contemplated rousing my father to confront the disturbance, a voice drifted from across the hallway—my father's voice, fervent and powerful. To my astonishment, he was praying aloud, his words a torrent of spiritual language that flowed from him like a river of faith. Each syllable twisted through the air, yet none penetrated my understanding. As the chaotic knocking faded, his voice filled the void, a beacon in the thickening darkness. I pressed my back against the wall, hands cradling my face, caught in a tempest of fear and shock. "God, please let this end," I whispered, intertwined with prayer, begging for release from my spiraling thoughts—a fervent wish to escape the treacherous clutches of seeming madness.

That afternoon, I confided in my mother, pouring out my fears that unseen demons preyed upon me now that I had finally dared to embrace happiness and healing. She enveloped me in a cocoon of comfort, her voice steady as she urged me to read Psalm 23 at dawn and dusk. Deep down, I sensed the shadows lurking were much more than mere side effects of medication. I'm not the kind of person who typically indulges in horror films or supernatural flicks. To be honest, I'm quite the scaredy-cat—terrified of the shadows that linger long after the credits roll. So these haunting dreams I keep experiencing are definitely not reflections of my natural everyday life. With my mother's wisdom intact, I decided to surrender my life to God's care. A woman of unwavering faith, my mother had prayed over me countless times, her intercessions resonating like soothing balm over my troubled soul. In a moment of vulnerability, I withheld how, during the first few times I borrowed her well-worn Bible, sheer electrical currents pulsed through my body, manifesting as uncontrollable shivers that raced through my limbs—the spirits within me writhing and fleeing as I yearned for the light.

"He shouted at the top of his voice, "What do you want with me, Jesus, Son of the Most High God? In God's name don't torture me!" For Jesus had said to him, "Come out of this man, you impure spirit!" He gave them permission, and the impure spirits came out and went into the pigs. The herd, about two thousand in number, rushed down the steep bank into the lake and were drowned."
Mark 5:7-8,13 NIV

"Be quiet!" Jesus said sternly. "Come out of him!" Then the demon threw the man down before them all and came out without injuring him. All the people were amazed and said to each other, "What words these are! With authority and power he gives orders to impure spirits and they come out!"
Luke 4:35-36 NIV

14 April 2023

The Lord is my shepherd and my savior. I've been repeating it because it is true. I believe he has bestowed patience in me. I must receive and show Him that I'm ready. My God is always beside me helping me. Thank you, God. Keep me confident and humble. I'm so excited you're always working in the shadows. You were right. You always are always. It's happening sooner than I thought. I feel happy. I deserve to be happy. You're always pushing me to be happy. You and my angels are always guiding me. I love you. I love you all. Thank you. Please continue to guide me with new lessons and love self love. I finally feel like I deserve it. My excitement and happy emotions are over the top. You continue to bless me and I need you to hear my praise. I am grateful. The new me is sad I couldn't be there for past Amber. But I'm finally looking forward and living in the present. Thank you for finally giving me the opportunity to prove my potential. You've always known who I was destined to be. Thank you! Thank you, thank you! I love this Amber. I love the other ones too but this version is my favorite. Thank you God, I shall receive graciously, in your precious name, amen

15 April 2023

It's only the following day. I'm still basking in the excitement and happiness. I'm so grateful. God you're so good to me. I really just wanted to talk with you. Have a nice little journal chat. It's been a while and my hand cramps up after a minute. I don't write like I used to in school. I'm old now too. LOL. I wanted to talk to you about a couple things, but I'm sure you already know my intentions and what they are. I will start with my friend Esther. I wanted to pray for her strength to open up more. I know she wants to but she is so scared. I really just want to help her get out of her comfort zone a little. It was fun messaging her crush for her, but she seemed so stressed out. I just pray for her confidence. Thanks. I pray that tomorrow goes well for her. Please show her a cautious way to go about this situation. Guide her. I pray that she listens. I pray that she sees the signs. If this is merely her practice person, I pray she succeeds and learns the lesson. You will always know more than me. I just want to bring her to you. I really do want him to like her. She deserves a good man. She's just scared. Please God, make it less challenging for her. I know time means nothing, but I'm begging for her to be given some mercy. If it's not meant to be, please be gentle on the letdown. I pray for her confidence and success... Secondly, I pray for my friend Tamar. With the drivers being let go often at work, I want her to succeed. Healed in all places that I may not know about and that her business becomes successful. We all deserve good things. I hope she stays excited about it all. Please protect her and guide her. I can tell she is one of your favorites as well. She is so kind and I really do feel like she is meant for so much more. I love that girl and I'm thankful you put her in my life. Thank you for putting all of these people in my life and for all the opportunities. Amen.

I had another dream last night. The devil was trying to get me, but the Lord, you are my savior and shepherd. It was an invisible figure, running on all fours, and hissing. I saw the prints in the ground as he ran around. A white figure, almost of light, started wrestling with the invisible being and was winning. Scene swap to me being stabbed repeatedly in the gut and questioned. "Why won't you die? In my mind, I knew I had Your strength in me. He gave up and said "I'll be back." I know he'll be back. He will wait until I'm desperate and vulnerable. He will come when I feel weak. God, please protect me. Watch over me. This new journey will be scary, but I don't doubt that I can do it. I know it will bring all challenges but I can't do it without you still. I'm ready only because I got you by my side. The next few weeks will be a patience game. The devil will try me at every moment. I'm well aware and sure that you know I don't want to fail. I always want to make you proud. Guide me to keep me on the right path. Please give me knowledge and strength and patience. Amen. I want to talk about one last thing.

I haven't talked about love in a while. God, please help me sort out my emotions and intentions. If you have placed James in my life for me, please give him the strength to bring it up to me. To let me know to entertain the thought and bring it to my awareness. I want you to help us take it slow. If it is meant to be, you've always known best for me...

Maybe I don't know because I don't feel like I deserve it. I deserve whatever good man you have in store for me. He seems like a really good guy. It was out of nowhere the feelings hit. I did miss him when he was gone. It wasn't a lie I told. He has a beautiful smile, especially when it's genuine. He's kind to me. He's generous. He's appreciative... Has money to provide... I'm actually crying, sorry. I'm emotionally in my closet again with tears in my eyes while writing.... My husband is kind. My husband is generous. My husband is loving. My husband provides... When you told me Paul didn't match the description. However, James does. I'm tired of thinking. I know what's next. I'm sorry. You know better. I shouldn't. If it is, thank you. If it isn't, thank you as well. I'm grateful for my current opportunities and career and self-love. You blessed me daily. Patience, love and success is what I felt ever since I've rid the devil off of my shoulders. I am loved by you. I love you. I am loved by you. I love you. Please don't allow me to pursue anything that is not for me. But also if it is for me, please show me the gift of receiving. I'm so happy at this point and I want everyone to share that with me. In your most precious name, amen.

16 April 2023

I think I'm thinking too much again. God, please keep me patient. I get excitable easily, but it's only because I know you have amazing things planned for me. Love comes when you least expect it. Now that I know it's coming, will you push it back? Will you deem me not ready? I keep thinking James will be my person next. I don't know, but I'm starting to like him. Am I his type? Am I interesting enough for him? Is he all about me? Does he serve and resonate with my highest good? Is he whom you want me with? I'm trying to calm myself. It is a lot, but I'm so happy. Is he my real twin flame/soulmate? Am I ready? I don't want to go back to who I was. James seems to be someone that knows what he wants. He has it together and is just waiting for the right one. I feel like you've given me many signs, but I'm so scared to be wrong. I do like him. I like him. I know I did when he smiled at me the first day of orientation. I couldn't explain it. He made me blush like a child. It was so different. Now, I just seen an image of us standing in the lobby of our current company and he's holding our baby. I'm holding the diaper bag. We're so in love with our baby. He/She is so cute. We're married and running the business together. He cares for me in ways, I know my past wouldn't have. God saved me from that. I am forever grateful. We can't stop looking at the baby and he looks at me and kisses me quickly. Everything feels like safe and like a home. I want that. I think I could finally admit that I wouldn't mind that with James. It's been a long journey that God has put us through. I'm thankful for whatever He does. His plan is the best plan. I pray this vision is Yours. Amen.

19 April 2023

I did it to myself. I think he has a girlfriend. God please tell me he doesn't. Should I ask him? Should I do that? Is that it? Do I need to ask him? To get it over with? I can just leave my job, if it ever gets weird. I don't have to stay. No more people pleasing. I should just ask him but that's so unprofessional. I don't care. I don't want to waste time. I could ask Jacob. Jacob would know. He talks to James every day. I'm tired of always waiting for my 'ten of pentacles' moment. They've fallen. What happened to my ten of pentacles? God, please I thought... it's crumbling... everything.

23 April 2023

I have a bit to write about. Well, one major thing and tiny things elsewhere. I'll talk about the small things first. I don't want to end my entry in a state of lack mentality. I didn't ask James yet. Something told me to hold off. I don't think I should plan it. It never goes as planned. Anyways. I should just go with the vibe. God has told me there is no rush. Feel it out. If I have anxiety it's probably not the right time. I worry about a lot though. The worst he could say to me is that he's not interested in me or that he has a girlfriend. And so, it is what it is. I will find someone else if it's not meant to be. God's rejection is also his protection. I said it a little wrong but you get the point. I wanted to mention how I think James is an Aquarius... He gives me those vibes. Weird! LOL. That's my boss. I don't know why or where this feeling came from. It is so random. The last thing I want to do is force something that isn't in the cards for me. God just told me I can't force him to do anything. That's true. I'm interested in getting to know him. God has been working behind the scenes a lot for me and I've just been sitting pretty lol. He told me that I can rest and receive. I don't have to put pressure on anything. It has felt quiet but I know he's just like I'm going to be right back. Just sit and don't do anything LOL. Sorry, I really am in a happy mood. I feel so good since my medication. I wish it happened sooner. Thank you for always having my side, Lord. I'd be lying if I said I didn't want James to be into me. For some reason, I want him to be so into me. Be my person. To learn and grow with. A real twin flame? Paul was probably my false twin. I don't know. It could just be a coincidence, but his eyes are also intense. Almost like Paul. It's hard to look at him. He's cute though. I wonder if he finds it hard to make eye contact with me. Are mine intense as well? Am I thinking too much on it? I'm sure I am. He doesn't look at me directly all that often, but when he does I feel my heart flutter. I pray I don't make him feel uncomfortable. I don't want him to be weird around me. I still like him as a person. I just fear a negative reaction. He might not be into me and I'm overthinking his weirdness right. He doesn't talk to anyone else like me. He's so calm when he's just with me. He's a good guy. I honestly don't think he does what he does for me for any other worker. He commands the others to do things, but he asks me for favors. I could be overthinking it and he just likes me as a worker. Okay, part of me fears he will be horrified that I like him. He will think he gave me signals and didn't intentionally try to. He's so nice to me and I think we could meet each other in the middle with a lot. I wonder if he feels the vibes I give him. He stands so close to me. I love it LOL. I'm the only one he touches. Appropriately of course. He's always ready and available to help me. He's not sarcastic with me. I feel so strange thinking about him this way. God, please help me sort out my emotions. God, keep me in your works. I don't want to ruin my promotion. If I am to ask him, I need a clear opening. I need him to be in a good mood. The last thing I need is to tell him while he's frustrated. I'm approaching him differently than I would anyone before.

I want to be blunt. I don't need to drop hints. I need him to know for sure. That way, he can decide if he wants to pursue me. I will not give my energy in going after a man. God has me receiving and so I shall. I know he's doing work in the background. It's not for me to figure out. I need to stop being scared of learning lessons, however, I don't want to mess up a good thing for myself. Trying to chase after love has gotten me nowhere. My career comes first and then love. However, I want him to know that he is on my mind as an interest. He can decide after. Okay. The big thing I wanted to talk about was my encounter with a ghost. She was very cool. I think she was concerned for me. I was taking midol medicine almost everyday for like 4 days. Along with my prescription. The caffeine began to make me talk in my sleep. I was having like three dreams a night talking in my sleep. On Wednesday, I didn't take any but I think the caffeine was still in my body. Around 4:40 a.m. I felt a double tap on my knee. Pause. My brain woke up and for some reason I thought it was my sister's bothering me. Double tap again. I fly up annoyed with whoever was waking me up. There was a silhouette figure. Of a young woman or lady. With her arms crossed in a waiting position, she faded quickly. I couldn't make out her face but she was on the shorter side, had her hair wrapped, and with a pleasant stance. My dad says it could have been his aunt's daughter. She passed in the house and it was probably in her sleep. I think she was concerned for me. After all of my dreams, she wanted to wake me up from talking. I'm grateful for her. I hope she knows I'm thankful. I hate talking in my sleep. I'm okay and I wonder if you are lingering, I hope you are doing well. I pray for your peace too.

Chapter 5

Cup Runneth Over

Psalms 23:1-6 NIV

[1] The Lord is my shepherd, I lack nothing.
[2] He makes me lie down in green pastures, he leads me beside quiet waters,
[3] he refreshes my soul. He guides me along the right paths for his name's sake.
[4] Even though I walk through the darkest valley, I will fear no evil, for you are with me; your rod and your staff, they comfort me.
[5] You prepare a table before me in the presence of my enemies. You anoint my head with oil; my cup overflows.
[6] Surely your goodness and love will follow me all the days of my life, and I will dwell in the house of the Lord forever.

Every single morning and evening, without fail, I would immerse myself in the reading and recitation of this Psalm, letting its comforting words wash over me like a calming ointment. At first, I couldn't shake the feeling of absurdity that crept in as I read aloud, a lingering self-consciousness gnawing at me. Yet, the desperation to reclaim a sense of "normal" drove me forward; I was willing to do anything to escape the shadows of madness that threatened my relationship with my family and friends. Meanwhile, the advice from my friends fluttered around me—suggestions about changing my medication—clashing with the reassurance I found in my sisters' validation, who had witnessed firsthand the tumult I endured through haunting visions and unsettling dreams as a child. As the sun dipped below the horizon on that pivotal first night, I wrapped myself in the pages of my mother's Bible, finding an unexpected tranquility that enveloped me like a maternal embrace. I fell asleep as if cradled by clouds, experiencing a profound stillness that chased away nightmares and fears.

The spiritual battle had raged fiercely before I surrendered my life to Christ, with the enemy striving relentlessly to snuff out my spirit. But then came God, a beacon of hope, dispatching His heavenly angels—guardians of my soul, illuminating my path because they knew the grand plans He held for my life. The forces of darkness sensed that once I grasped my true identity, the strength of knowing to whom I belonged would be a force to be reckoned with. My faith became an unyielding fortress; I became quick to answer whenever the voice of God called. Admittedly, there were moments when my human nature wrestled with reluctance and hesitation, but each time, I reminded myself gently yet firmly that His way is indeed the best way. With resolve, I would seize my cross—not in defeat, but with the determination to march boldly into the future. Reflecting, in April 2023, the catalyst for transformation began when I gave my life to Christ Jesus. From that point onward, an incredible metamorphosis took root within me. Just two months later, I experienced a divine deliverance from the clutches of witchcraft, astrology, tarot, and all deceitful Jezebel spirits that had shadowed my existence for far too long. Miraculously, three months passed, and though I found myself in a car accident—emerging unscathed—God truly blessed me, gifting me with a new vehicle as He swept away remnants of my old life, casting aside everything that held the memories of my time in "Egypt." Four months in, I ventured to Texas for a Prophetic Women's Conference, where prophetic words were spoken over my life—words declaring that God would plant me like a steadfast foundation, meant to stand strong for generations yet to come. As the seasons changed, six months later, the light of God's grace illuminated my heart as I found complete deliverance from the chains of depression and anxiety that sought to bind me. In an act of faith, I stepped away from my medication, realizing that He alone could serve as my Comforter. His miracles unfolded before me—miracles that reached even those on the precipice of despair, those who feel like they have no will to live. He held me in His embrace when I believed I was beyond saving, unveiling a vibrant life filled with love and abundance promised in His sacred word. He named me prophetess, and in this calling, I serve our Most High God with all the reverence and unreserved love my heart can muster.

During those tender moments, my heart was utterly enraptured by the divine presence of God. He painted hearts in the clouds, sending vivid reminders of His steadfast love and infinite attention to the smallest details of my life. Reflecting on my high school days, I remember the unfulfilled longing to attend the prom, held captive by my insecurities. Yet, in His mercy, God crafted a beautiful alternative for me—an ethereal opportunity to dress up, dance with a joyful spirit, and celebrate in honor of Him, enveloped in purity and grace. In that divine act, He restored every fragment of my heart that had been bruised by previous disappointments.

"Before I formed you in the womb I knew you, before you were born I set you apart; I appointed you as a prophet to the nations."
Jeremiah 1:5 NIV

4 May 2023

I did it earlier. Something told me to write again. I'm trying to tune into my intuition, my gut, not my mind. Satan kills all good through the mind. That's why he tried to send his demons after me.

You can't kill me. God is my protector and savior. I'm no longer on your team. God always wins. Well, I was really wanting to write about what I had done today. I'm proud of myself and I should be. I was so scared, but I wanted to step out on faith. I give it all to God. I told James today! I asked if he had a girlfriend, so now he knows I'm interested. He isn't making it weird. Weird. I feel like he was trying to comfort me. I was horrified LOL. I don't know why. I thought he would be horrified. Well, I was worried he wouldn't like me hitting on him. My old fears of being the " ugly, fat, black" girl to him, tortured me. The devil tried to stop me from living my life so many times. Not anymore. So he knows now. I knew he had a girlfriend, I wanted the confirmation from him. He's honest. I knew I could trust him. I want to let go. I want to believe God has told me that I've done a good thing and my life will undergo a change. It's out of my control. I need it to let go of me. I stewed over him having a girlfriend. I told myself it would have been better if he didn't have one. Honestly, it probably wouldn't. He seems like the person to really think over his options. His decisions take a lot of thought. He's studious, smart, intelligent, thoughtful, generous, caring, loving, knows what he wants, a protector, mature, charming, patient, kind, has his head on straight, a provider, and with a great sense of humor. He can and knows when to be serious. He is many things. The first time I can ever say that I have a lot to write about someone. I truly see him. I see all his good aspects. Maybe there are some bad. He hasn't given me any red flag vibes. I've told God that I don't want to seem to wish ill on anyone. I am happy for him that he's in a relationship. I hope he's happy, but if he isn't happy, I pray that God leads him to his happiness. Not saying that is with me, but God knows more than me. I have got to learn to let go of control. Control. It's not my job to worry over things like that and God has provided time and time again that He has it all under control. I have literally felt Him working in my life and He doesn't want me overwhelmed. I still have to enjoy the little things, but they are coming. I know. God has promised me and I just need to let go. The opportunity was literally handed to me today. I was patient and was given proper timing. It couldn't have been more perfect. It was slower today in business. God gave me the confidence for today. I told myself if he's in a good mood, I'll do it.

As soon as I was walking up front, contemplating over when he would come. He comes around the corner smiling, looking so handsome. I thought he had a haircut. Something was different about him today. His personality makes him adorable. Handsome really. I honestly had the heart eyes when I saw him coming. He is refreshing and has such good energy. He makes me excited to work. I do love my job as is, but when he left for those two weeks, I'm telling you, I didn't know how much that would affect me. I was kind of sad, but I wasn't aware of my feelings then. Until he came back and out of nowhere. I told him that I missed him. I did! I didn't know I would say it though LOL. James is so adorable and all of the above. He seems like he gets me. He understands my mind. We work well together. I was so scared of jeopardizing that. I think it's okay. Can I say this? Should I say this? I will say this... Something is telling me that he is my real twin. I won't label anything because he is my boss, but he feels like a puzzle piece. Him and Tamar both. They feel like they are a part of my soulmate season. People supporting my highest good. They are supportive and encouraging. A new start. I can breathe and let go now. Rest, you have done well is what my soul says. Keep doing what you're doing. Be patient and let go of fear and control. Do not rush and fear no evil. The Lord is my shepherd. I shall not want. My favorite Bible verse that has protected me. I feel my new beginnings and I trust God in his plans. With all the signs being shown I have no fear.

6 May 2023

"I gotta write!" I just jumped up. I wasn't asleep, but I just had another realization. I've had so many recently. It's my turn. God, I trust you. I trust you with everything I have. I will remain patient for you and your guidance. Thank you for all and everything. You told me to write and it'll all make sense... It's starting to make sense. My realization is another piece of the puzzle. My husband.... I asked for someone kind of obsessed with me, not in a toxic way, but someone that is crazy about me. He fits the description. I'm having a good time by not forcing anything. No worries. I know you've got my back. Almost a year to two years ago I was writing to you about my husband. I felt you hug me in the closet. I know you were there with me. You kept telling me Paul wasn't the one. I'm hearing false twin flame a lot now in regards to Paul. I think he was my false twin. Gave me the illusion of runner/chaser, but the toxic version. A love story, not a life story. However, my husband is the opposite. My husband adores me. My husband is patient and nurturing with me. My husband is caring and listens to me. My husband provides for me. My husband always chooses me over the others, happily. My husband wants to build with me. Me. He wants to start a family in the right way with me. Marriage, home, happiness, children. My husband understands me without judgment. My husband isn't afraid to take leaps of faith and prays with me. My husband is an amazing man and father. I love my husband. We've grown in true steady love. My husband is here. My husband will learn his lessons. I don't have to fight. Follow the Lord's guidance and I'm trusted with my intuition. God and his angels are watching over me. Continue to do as you are doing. Do not doubt or fear. Be yourself. Live in the moment and believe that you already have it all. God clears all the kinks. It's not my place to worry. My husband is here. James is my husband... God continue to protect me and him. It is not my place to worry how he gets to me. I hope he gets to me safely. Without pain. Without too much pain. Guard his heart in this battle that he may or may not be ready for. Allow him to go where he is happy. Show him the way, Lord. The way you have shown me. My husband who I am so thankful for. I know when we close the gap, all the pain will be worth it. I understand now. Thank you. Continue to show us Your way. Amen.

21 May 2023

Where to start? I was in a car accident. My first car accident on Thursday. Scary! I don't really need to write the details. I know God was in that car with me. My anxiety has heightened since then. I will not worry. Everything is working out. God will provide for me. Worry is the opposite of faith. I have faith and all is well. Thank you for delivering me from anxiety. That makes me want to talk about Friday, which I think I should. It's a segway into why I honestly needed to write. I was having a panic attack and I honestly believe it was another spiritual attack. While I was vulnerable, they came for me. I was doing fine until my coworker started talking about James possibly proposing to his current girlfriend. I started to feel sick physically. Out of nowhere I wanted to run home. She doesn't know how I honestly feel about him. She won't ever know, unless God works it out in a healthy way. I feel like I'm already in new lessons. I must stay true in my endeavors. My gut and heart is telling me to continue regardless of outcome. Let go of the outcome. Tell no one your plans. My mind is saying to ask if I should do this. He has a girlfriend and this feels wrong. Leave him alone. The devil can only get to me in my mind. The angels have been helping me though. I get signs and small progressions and confirmations. Then my mind just tells me that this is his personality and you're "looking too into" it. It couldn't be his personality because it's only mostly with me. He's gentle with me, caring, patient, does things for me. I don't have to fight for it. I feel so safe when he's here. When he's here with me. My sister laughed when I told her he was my safe haven. I said I was joking, but she knows I wasn't. Every time he leaves, something happens to me. He doesn't stand up my butt all day, but I feel confident and so safe when he's around. It feels so wrong to think like that of my boss. My boss with a girlfriend... That doesn't mean God wanted them together. We've all been in relationships we've stayed in just because it was easier than being lonely. This is where my downfall begins though. I feel evil, hoping and wishing the worst. I know that's my ego. I want him happy. I have a pure soul. I want him happy. Always go where you're happy. Where you're appreciated and loved. I'd rather tell my feelings than never say anything. I pray for courage. I've really been enjoying life a lot more. I love life and truly the journey is very fun for me. I don't want to obsess over the outcome. It will come if it's supposed to. Amen.

26 May 2023

I was getting tired so I wanted to write before bed. It was a good Friday. I have a big topic I want to write about because no one will believe me. They will make me doubt my intuition, however, I feel it in my gut and God has shown me the end goal. Not really an end but a gift for me. He showed me at the end of the path. They won't believe me, so I won't tell them but Tamar knows. James is very aware that I like him. I asked him yesterday if his girlfriend treats him well. He said yes. That's a good thing. I'm happy she does! No, it didn't go as I wanted, but I've gotten a little closer to him. Every time and every day is a new thing. I'm just having fun learning about him and semi crushing on him. I trust God's timing. I don't need to put my opinions in anything. God showed me who my husband is. He showed me a best friend that is so very loving and gives me all the attention. Compliments me mentally instead of physically. Confides in my opinions and fixes anything that's broken for me. Helps me in a time of need. Funny, intelligent, wise, caring, exciting to be around. So handsome. So so handsome to me. Only gives me attention. Doesn't talk to other women the way he talks to me. Tunnel vision all for me. And actually cares for me. Mildly obsessed but never too clingy, generous, happy, healthy, comfortable in the silence. The whole package! Has money and a great taste in music! It makes sense. James is my husband. God blessed me with what I could have if I follow Him. Believe in my intuition and faith. I will. It's not my job to put an opinion on anything. God may not want them together and who am I to argue with Him? I want to do it right this time. I don't want to be scared to fall in love hard anymore. James is so sweet. They called me delusional and obsessed. I want to humbly prove them wrong. God has my back. Always. Too many good things and syncs has happened to me, non-stop, to let me know. I'm on the correct path. I just have to keep going.

Psalm 23 <3

2 June 2023

Peace. The way I feel now. I'm sitting at the beach feeling so blessed and loved by God. Peace is like being in the middle of a storm and finding shelter. Peace isn't the absence of chaos. It's the presence of chaos and finding sanctuary in it. I have a lot to talk about and I don't even know where to start. I feel like I'm on God's path. Finally. I'm not forcing anything on my own and I feel like so much is happening and changing. I love every moment and day. The past few weeks I've learned so much about life. I feel excited for what's to come next, but I'm also enjoying every minute of the present and knowing God is watching and protecting me. The days seem to just flow by. The promise to bring heaven on earth is and will be fulfilled. Fulfilled! The way I feel gives me a confidence to my knowing and faith. I just had the most blessed experience. Two girls came up to me and my friend, Esther, to talk about the love of Christ! I knew we were supposed to meet. My confirmation. My approval to keep going. I'm finally on my way. Thank you, God. I finally love life. I love life. Thank you for your deliverance. The past few weeks have been a learning experience. Amen! Yesterday, I asked for your permission to pursue. I've been taking all the signs without asking you directly. I may not supposed to go after it. I feel like the Holy Spirit told me that it was safe to hope on this side.

26 June 2023

Jesus is waking me up. This time next year, I will be pregnant with a son. This will be my testimony. I have many already, but write and it'll all make sense. Thank you, God. This is the moment all of those tears were for. This moment I cry in joy. I send comfort to the old me that I can now lay to rest. Amen. She is okay now. Tears of sorrow are no longer. Tears of joy is the new beginning. Here I am, sitting at the side of my bed on the floor writing about what God told me. I love crazy faith. I will always turn to You, Father. You put me to sleep because I would try to mess it up. Thank You, Jesus! We are ready to follow You. Lord, I will continue to speak over my marriage and love for You. I accept Your transformation. I am ready! Amen.

31 August 2023

My God. My God. My Father. For I love you. You! Lord of all Lords. King of all Kings. The most high God! I loveth thee! My month of breakthrough. The month you opened the heavens for me. The month in which the heavens truly rejoiced and celebrated. The days leading up to my trip were good. I was so excited because I felt as if something miraculous was about to happen. Thank you! God, you did it! I remember asking for you to open the heavens. You open them. God, I love you! You! Oh, I have so much to write about. Before my trip, work was still going well. Me and James had a busy Monday and Tuesday. Wednesday was busy too but we had a co-worker there. Last week, Father, you wanted me to make cards promoting the application at our job. I loved every moment. We had 20 applicants! No one, but you! I only took down the cards because we started to get some negative feedback. James didn't want to tell me while I was on break. A sweet man he is. And he didn't want to tell my sister either. LOL. Father, I told him that he could have told me! I was so scared. Someone threw them out! Father have mercy on your son. I think he is starting to see. He is worried about his dog now. I know he loves his dog though. Keep him safe and heal him. Please. For James knows not what he does. His dog is probably the only thing that gave him love and comfort through his painful years. Just from the things I have learned through him.

Now back to the trip! It was life-changing. I would do it all over if I could. I prayed that I didn't want to be scared anymore. I went to the altar, kneeled, and prayed. You then wanted me to dance for you. I wanted to cry then and there. I was handed a purple sheet and spun in circles. My gift of royalty. Father, I will dance for you anywhere. I love you! Always and forever. I adore you. I met the most loving sisters ever there. All I can hear is, "He sees you and He loves you." Becca, my closest sister. I love her. All will be invited to my wedding. The support and love were stronger than blood family. That Saturday was even better. Prophet Amires told me to dance and she prophesied and spoke over me. I danced. I was told that I had a mark over my life. I was so happy. I was sleeping in a cabin named "Happiness." All was well. I caught the Holy Ghost and couldn't stop praising. God, you did it. You did it. Gala night was better than any prom I could have ever went to. Beautiful red dresses and we were all loving God. Heaven was open. Blessings began to fall. I spoke in tongues on the way home. However, before I went home, I drove to my "home" church. Transformation Church in Tulsa, Oklahoma. Pastor Charles confirmed it all. Everyone was so nice. I told my testimony to two women and was so close to them. Real women of God. Every second felt like the heavens were gifting me. Christmas for sure came early! God! Thank you! You! I keep writing lowercase. Father, You know my heart! I am a new me in confidence and love. Prayers were answered all weekend. When I got back, I was so excited to tell my parents. They knew I was changed. Yesterday, when I got to work. I believe James was so happy to see me. He was so stressed without me. He was about to quit! He was fed up. Fed up! My poor coworker was probably so scared LOL. It was only two days of me being gone! LOL. He feels it too. Most of the afternoon today, we sat and watched the news together. He was very teary-eyed today again too. I wonder what he is thinking. Are they sleepy tears or happy? Loving tears? I love that man . Father, thank you for trusting me with his heart. I promise to hold it close. He means so much to me and I look up to him at this point. I know something was different when I came back. He just wanted to be around me constantly. My husband. My husband. I love you, husband. I can't wait for our future following Christ. Amen, Amen, and Amen.

Chapter 6

Warfare Among Family

It was in the early whispers of February 2024 that God gently revealed His plan to me, one that would take me far from my familiar life—my family, friends, and job. By March, the specifics unfolded; I found myself bound for Tulsa, Oklahoma, destined to worship and serve at Transformation Church. This sacred place had been a guiding light for me since I first gave my life to Christ, and the community there has remarkably transformed my heart and mind. The memory of my visit six months before God's whisper remains etched in my mind, especially the sermon on the importance of fostering connections within a community of faith. Unbeknownst to me then, this congregation was to become my new home. My journey culminated over the Resurrection weekend, from March 29 to April 1, when I arrived at my promised land, ready to embark on a new season with God—armed with the wisdom and strength He had instilled in me during my wilderness trials. My solitary first outing led me to a quaint local park, inviting me to unwind as I wandered along its peaceful paths. The sight of a serene pond inhabited by graceful geese, surrounded by vibrant fields blanketed with blossoms and lush green grass, filled my soul with tranquility. In that moment, the Holy Spirit stirred within me, a gentle reminder that He makes me lie down in green pastures, leads me beside still waters, and refreshes my spirit. He guides my steps along the right paths for His name's sake, and it was then that I broke into tears of joy, knowing without a doubt that I had arrived exactly where I was meant to be.

As the time approached for my long-anticipated journey into the promised land, an intense surge of spiritual warfare loomed over me like a dark cloud, casting shadows on my path. The backward spirit, a relentless adversary, roamed freely, and I found myself woefully unprepared for the ferocity of the attacks that lay ahead. There was an undercurrent of resistance from my family, a fierce opposition to my decision to heed God's call. It wasn't a battle against them, I reassured myself, but rather a struggle within my own heart—a clash against fear, uncertainty, and the persistent worry that threatened to choke my resolve. In that pivotal time, my faith stood resolute, bolstered by God's meticulous preparation and pruning, designed specifically for the trials that were to come. Yet, mere weeks before my departure from the familiarity of home, I experienced a moment of vulnerability when pride crept in unexpectedly, stealthy and insidious.

That week became a whirlwind of distractions—a cacophony of tactics and strategies devised to keep me from my purpose, to test my tenacity, to teach me valuable lessons, and to lead me further along my divine path, guiding me to my kairos moment. I wrestled with my mounting pride, the origin of which remained elusive. God, in His wisdom, had chosen not to unveil the source, reminding me time and again through subtle nudges and profound lessons that my faith needed to shine untainted by the shadows of this world. I was learning that peace and purpose often emerged from the very battles we least expected to face. God had repeatedly warned me about the dangers of associating too closely with my youngest sister, whose worldly influence threatened to extinguish the flickering flame of faith I clung to.

My youngest sister has always been my shadow, dutifully following in my footsteps until the moment I began to heal. It was as if a line had been drawn in the sand; she stood resolute on the other side, refusing the very lifeline I sought to extend. I was perplexed, caught up in the whirlpool of my own emotions, unable to comprehend why she resisted the chance to heal alongside me. After all, we have perpetually been two peas in a pod, inseparable through the fabric of our lives. She, the keeper of my secrets, the guardian of my innermost thoughts and lingering pains. We had shared the same cramped room for years, a sacred space filled with whispers, laughter, and the occasional tears. Our resemblance was uncanny, reflected not only in our features but in our souls, creating a bond that defied explanation. We never engaged in the petty quarrels that often plague siblings; conflict felt like a distant concept to us. Never did a raised voice cross between us in anger. I don't care what anyone claims; when you genuinely love someone, the idea of inflicting physical pain is a curse to that deep connection. What we shared was, and always what I thought would be real love. Genuine love—not the fleeting kind that people often toss around like confetti, but a steadfast, unyielding bond that felt woven into the very fabric of who we were.

"Love is patient, love is kind. It does not envy, it does not boast, it is not proud. It does not dishonor others, it is not self-seeking, it is not easily angered, it keeps no record of wrongs. Love does not delight in evil but rejoices with the truth. It always protects, always trusts, always hopes, always perseveres. Love never fails. But where there are prophecies, they will cease; where there are tongues, they will be stilled; where there is knowledge, it will pass away."
1 Corinthians 13:4-8 NIV

I delve into this topic more thoroughly in a blog post, but let me clarify: my intention is not to tarnish her name or dismantle her reputation. In truth, this experience will someday form an integral part of her testimony, just as it is currently a fundamental aspect of my own narrative. I often found myself pondering, especially in my past when I wasn't in communion with God, about why someone would keep returning to a relationship marked by domestic violence. It baffled me to think that love could run so deep that it would permit harm and manipulation to flourish, that one could accept hollow apologies dripping with remorse and confusion. The cries of anguish—"I don't know what happened," they lament, as if the storm within them had appeared unexpectedly—are familiar echoes. "It doesn't excuse my behavior, but no one reassured me, and I was just so worried for you," they insist, trying to weave a narrative that softens their guilt. "I just got angry," they say, as if those words could erase the marks left behind. "I know I messed up, but please, don't stop talking to me," they plea, caught in the vicious cycle of "love" that strays riskily close to destruction. It's a tale as old as time, and yet it unfolds anew in the lives of so many, each version a haunting reflection of hope intertwined with despair. The turbulent spirit dwelled within her, a tempest I had sensed brewing since I was saved. I often found myself muttering in frustration, "She is the Cain to my Able," as the shadows of jealousy morphed into something more sinister. Every act of progress I made, every triumph in my healing journey, was met with her cutting remarks, sharp as a blade, aimed directly at my heart to bring me low. It was as if, wherever jealousy took root, it unleashed a malevolent host, awakening spirits of every dark persuasion, swirling together in a cacophony of bitterness and spite. Her words, laced with poison, wrapped around me like a noose, threatening to strangle the light I had fought so hard to nurture within.

"For where you have envy and selfish ambition, there you find disorder and every evil practice."
James 3:16 NIV

He opened my eyes to a profound truth: my strength was tethered to Him, and without His guidance, I would be adrift. My youngest sister—the one whom I cherished and often referred to as my twin since my early memories at the tender age of four—how could I ever consider leaving her behind? Yet, as if whispering directly into my heart, God has illuminated the path for me, urging me to distance myself for far too long, and my reluctance to heed that call had sparked the conflict leading to our painful confrontation. In that room filled with emotional turmoil, I recognized the undeniable truth—He was absolutely right (of course!). The time for trauma bonding under the guise of love was over. I understood that if I failed to walk in step with my Creator, I risked placing her upon the very pedestal that belonged to my God. To turn back to her, I realized, would mean sacrificing my destiny, my promised land. In the days that followed, the haunting question, "What did I do to deserve this?" spun relentlessly in my mind, a relentless tormentor I struggled to silence. Each passing hour after our rift, I could hear Jesus, so tender and patient, asking me gently, "Are you okay?" My truthful reply would sometimes be a simple, "Yes," while other moments would crack open the facade, revealing a softer "Not really." I managed to forgive her for myself; our compassionate Father had extended His grace towards me, yet somehow, forgiving myself remained an insurmountable obstacle. How ironic it felt to let my pride overshadow my growth after such intense spiritual pruning. The whole ordeal left me questioning not only how it could unfold this way but also why it was necessary at all. Despite this painful chapter, my love for my sister remains steadfast, and I will continue to lift her up in prayer, keeping watch over her spirit. She is in the process of healing, and I trust that nothing is unattainable when set against the infinite power of my God.

"For if you forgive other people when they sin against you, your heavenly Father will also forgive you. But if you do not forgive others their sins, your Father will not forgive your sins. "
Matthew 6:14-15 NIV

12 March 2024

The Lord is gracious and merciful. The Lord is gracious and merciful. He knew the things that would happen. He loves and cares for your promise because it isn't just about you, but about His purpose. His purpose to bring the loss to the found. You are not perfect. It is okay. I am sorry for not listening, father. I repent for still hanging out with her and not saying no. I'm saying no from now on. I want to say no to everyone, but I will use my given discernment. I have much to be appreciative for. Thank you for saving me and handling the cop also. You did not have to. What a day!? I still have to go back to work tomorrow afternoon. Honestly, I may need a week from that. Gosh, give me strength, Papa. My heart won't be able to handle tomorrow without You. God, what was today? The devil was literally after me! She was with me. You were right. I don't have the same provision when I'm with her or anyone with them attached. All the crying started to make me mad so I had to leave. I didn't show it though. Papa, please I will definitely leave her alone now. I'm not getting beat up again. The enemy was so mad he couldn't stop what God was doing so he decided to fight me. OKAY! I know the literal blood, sweat, and tears it took to get to my promise. You cannot stop this! Give up Satan! I still can't believe it honestly. What a crazy day. Papa... Jesus.... How? I'm not testing that ever again, but I know my blessings are about to be abundant. I love You. Thank You. I was in such disbelief that I didn't know what to say. I just heard myself say, "You told me." Papa, please forgive her. Please forgive her. Forgiveness does not mean reentrance of course. My heart is secure in You and on lock! I don't care what anybody thinks. My blessings are coming and I will rejoice in You for being faithful. Signs that God has answered my prayers... Hell is breaking loose. God has already won the fight. It feels like the world is against me most of the time. God is for me. Therefore no one can stand against me. Please God. I truly beg for Your vindication. I never said I wanted to fight alone. This is Your fight. Why am I going through this? Was there not enough breaking in the past? I'm leaving. I'm going. I'm done. No more. I don't want to hurt anymore. Please, Papa. Please let my vindication come earlier than 3 weeks from now. I'm losing blood trying to hold on. I know it's my fault.

18 March 2024

I need Your protection, Jesus, for when the devil comes. Come trying to start something with temptation or anything like incorrect knowledge or trying to test my character, I may need You to remind me who I am. Hold my hand into the next area. I don't want to get too comfortable here. Endings just mean new beginnings. After the tears I have sown, I pray that I will reap in joy. As it says in Psalm 126. Long suffering is your salvation. God has something planned and I don't know what it is, but I know it will be worth the wait. After all the years of toiling for love, money, joy, peace. I know the goodness of God. He is leading me to something I couldn't imagine. I have my faith in Him. God will provide everything for me. He is my provider. I need no one else. No one else. Only God and I. Lord, I trust You. Isaiah 35...

Amber, you will surely reap in joy.

Chapter 7

Entering The Promised Land

I stand as a living testament to the profound goodness of the Lord and the fulfillment of His promises in my life. This book serves as a heartfelt testimony, chronicling the miraculous ways in which God has saved and transformed me. His unwavering willingness and desire to do the same for you is as certain as the dawn. It was during Resurrection Weekend that I made a bold leap of faith, physically stepping into my promised land, a moment charged with divine significance. I draw inspiration from Abraham, the epitome of faith and a cherished friend of God; his journey mirrors my own as I traverse the path he once walked. Together, we share the understanding that faith can indeed move mountains, opening doors to the blessings that await us. With each page, I invite you into this story, a narrative woven with threads of grace and redemption, where the adventure of faith unfolds for us all.

"By faith Abraham, when called to go to a place he would later receive as his inheritance, obeyed and went, even though he did not know where he was going. By faith he made his home in the promised land like a stranger in a foreign country; he lived in tents, as did Isaac and Jacob, who were heirs with him of the same

promise. For he was looking forward to the city with foundations, whose architect and builder is God."
Hebrews 11:8-10 NIV

In the face of formidable challenges, I steadfastly chose to follow God, embracing His will as a guiding light in my life each and every day. The skepticism and harsh words of those around me—individuals who doubted my divine connection and questioned whether God truly walked beside me—sought to dismantle my spirit completely. Yet, through the struggle and turmoil, I emerged unscathed, a testament to the power of His redemptive grace. I stand here, living proof of His profound ransom, a beacon of hope and resilience forged in faith amidst the storm. Each step I took was marked by unwavering courage, as I navigated a world filled with doubt and disbelief, only to find my footing on the solid ground of His love and purpose.

"Just as the Son of Man did not come to be served, but to serve, and to give his life as a ransom for many."
Matthew 20:28 NIV

I am not here because of my own deeds but through steadfast faith in Christ. It is this profound relationship that has paved my way to this moment; nothing else could have carried me here. Reflecting on the years spent toiling under the notion that constant performance equates to love or validates one's existence feels utterly draining. How grateful I am to recognize that God's love is not contingent upon my actions, whether they be grand or minimal. The burdensome weights I once bore fall away when I choose to trust in Him. He is an unfaltering lifeguard for His children—never allowing them to drown amidst the turbulent waters of life. As I stood on the threshold of my journey towards the promised land, I felt an unsettling wave of nerves wash over me. Doubt crept into my heart, fear echoing ominously within. Yet, in the depths of my soul, I understood that I was on the right path, guided by His divine word. In moments of quiet reflection and earnest prayer, I reached out to God, seeking both reassurance and guidance. It was then that He spoke to my spirit from the scripture—Isaiah 35 resonated deeply with my concerns and hopes. Verses 8-10 took special hold of me, their messages weaving comfort and strength into my very being. They reminded me not only of the beauty that lies ahead but also of the joy that comes when we lean into faith, trusting wholly in His everlasting love and promises.

"And a highway will be there; it will be called the Way of Holiness; it will be for those who walk on that Way. The unclean will not journey on it; wicked fools will not go about on it. No lion will be there, nor any ravenous beast; they will not be found there. But only the redeemed will walk there, and those the LORD has rescued will return. They will enter Zion with singing; everlasting joy will crown their heads. Gladness and joy will overtake them, and sorrow and sighing will flee away."
Isaiah 35:8-10 NIV

The highway known as the Way of Holiness is destined for those who dare to walk upon it, a path illuminated by the light of faith. I unwaveringly tread the Way of Christ, each step drawing me closer to the highway that leads to the vibrant land of the living. God's promise shines before me, a home overflowing with milk and honey —a sanctuary filled to the brim with His boundless favor and unfathomable love. This bounty is mine as long as I adhere to His commandments: to love the Lord with unwavering devotion, to walk in obedience to His will, and to cling tenaciously to Him as spoken in Deuteronomy 11. Leaving behind everything I held dear in my quaint hometown was not a simple feat, yet the hand of God was upon me, preparing my heart long before my departure. He whispered the secrets of trust into my spirit, reminding me that not all who surround us harbor our best interests. The human heart can often veer toward selfishness, and the mind can falter when confronted with the vastness of the Lord's divine ways. It is a shame

—family members, those nearest to us, can sometimes unknowingly become the very shackles that bind us, their emotions urging us to stay hidden in familiar shadows rather than venture into the freedom of the unknown. Nonetheless, I stand tall as one who has been redeemed, my feet firmly planted in Zion, my promised land, where I enter with songs of praise and a joy that knows no end. The New International Version has always been my cherished translation; it is the first I reach for whenever I seek wisdom and guidance. Yet, prompted by the gentle nudging of the Spirit, I found myself delving into the King James Version, exploring its rich, poetic cadence, and so I embraced it with an open heart. I recognized that both paths could unite in harmony, each revealing aspects of God's truth uniquely illuminating my journey.

"And an highway shall be there, and a way, and it shall be called The way of holiness; the unclean shall not pass over it; but it shall be for those: the wayfaring men, though fools, shall not err therein . No lion shall be there, nor any ravenous beast shall go up thereon, it shall not be found there; but the redeemed shall walk there: and the ransomed of the LORD shall return, and come to Zion with songs and everlasting joy upon their heads: they shall obtain joy and gladness, and sorrow and sighing shall flee away."

Isaiah 35:8-10 KJV

At the time of immersing myself in those pages, I failed to grasp the significance of why I needed to delve into both versions of the text. On this unmarked highway toward my promise, deep in the heart of my journey, I found myself echoing the profound words of verse 10 in the KJV: "and the ransomed of the Lord shall return, and come to Zion with songs." Each syllable reverberated in my spirit, a call both timely and timeless. It was an early Saturday morning, the dawning sun casting its golden glow on March 30, 2024, exactly one year since the divine whispered His call for me to be His humble servant. With purpose burning in my heart, I eagerly set my course for Tulsa, Oklahoma. There, I felt the spirit of God all around me, low and sweet, speaking of a land flowing with milk and honey—an abundant paradise. This land of promise, nourished by the rains from the heavens, is where the Almighty places His unwavering gaze, tending to it with love and care from the dawn of the year until its final days. After much spiritual wandering, I crossed the Jordan River's threshold on that glorious day, a physical testament to the journey I had undertaken in the spirit. I am truly one of the ransomed of the Lord, released from the bleak existence I once endured in my hometown. Now, I wear a crown of joy upon my head, an emblem of triumph where my former sorrows and sighs have taken flight. As I glided past the 'Welcome to Oklahoma' sign, an overwhelming wave of the Spirit enveloped me like a warm embrace. In that sacred moment, relief washed over me as I realized I had been liberated from every shackle binding me to spirits that dwell in shadows—fear that once gripped my heart, the pain that colored my days, the poverty that hovered over me like a cloud, lust, coveting, dissatisfaction, despair, and countless others began to dissipate in the radiant name of Jesus. In His graciousness, He was revealed to me by the one true God.

Let me assure you, there is not a single blessing He has bestowed upon me that He wouldn't generously offer to you, dear reader. We, the beloved children of God, are endowed with every provision we could ever need, rendering us devoid of lack. Should you find yourself yearning or sensing an emptiness within, it is a sign that you have yet to fully embrace the glorious gift of the Living Water. Call upon Him to dwell within you, and attentively follow the sacred commands of our Lord. Jesus is not merely our Savior; He longs to reign as your Lord. A Lord who rules your life desires your utmost good and yearns to guide you toward maturity in the Spirit—do not turn away from Him, the unshakeable foundation beneath your feet. Always carry with you the irreplaceable gift of mercy and grace bestowed upon us from our heavenly Father. Mercy, that sweet delay from getting what we rightfully deserve, and grace, the extravagant blessing of receiving what we could never earn. Our King, our loving Father, paid the ultimate price for our souls with His only begotten Son so that we might experience life in all its fullness, a life where we can walk, talk, dance, and truly live in His presence. So, thank You, Jesus, for Your boundless sacrifice of love—a love unfathomable to the mortal heart. May we steadfastly pursue our Lord, Savior, and Leader in all our days, embracing the adventure He offers in every moment we walk beside Him.

"Large crowds were traveling with Jesus, and turning to them he said: "If anyone comes to me and does not hate father and mother, wife and children, brothers and sisters—yes, even their own life—such a person cannot be my disciple. And whoever does not carry their cross and follow me cannot be my disciple. "Suppose one of you wants to build a tower. Won't you first sit down and estimate the cost to see if you have enough money to complete it? For if you lay the foundation and are not able to finish it, everyone who sees it will ridicule you, saying, 'This person began to build and wasn't able to finish.' "Or suppose a king is about to go to war against another king. Won't he first sit down and consider whether he is able with ten thousand men to oppose the one coming against him with twenty thousand? If he is not able, he will send a delegation while the other is still a long way off and will ask for terms of peace. In the same way, those of you who do not give up everything you have cannot be my disciples. "Salt is good, but if it loses its saltiness, how can it be made salty again? It is fit neither for the soil nor for the manure pile; it is thrown out. "Whoever has ears to hear, let them hear."

Luke 14:25-35 NIV

30 March 2024

I have officially and physically crossed over! God is so good. Papa, I don't know where the funds are going to come from, but please don't have me looking foolish. I don't want to be embarrassed. I'm going to have to ask for money. Papa... Why? My pride needs to be torn down. But You called me to this. They aren't going to think it was You then. Who do I have to ask? Please don't make me ask, James. I hate asking for money. I wish I just had my own. Whatever! I am in my promised land. I feel like a stranger right now, but soon enough I believe my husband will be with me. My husband come on please. Monday is his test. Oh I pray for good results. I pray that he will miss me. In the same way, I miss him. Come back to me. I now feel more alone than when I was back home. God? Abraham was a strong man. He had family with him too, right? I don't have family so I'm just alone. It is well. And I will be well soon enough. The promise will be here.

18 April 2024

I am grateful that I am blessed by God. I thank You. The way that I know I'm blessed. I'm not in a physical home, but he protects me because I dwell in His house all the days of my life. He protects me in all his ways. I live righteously in Jesus Christ. I live a repented life. My heart belongs to the Lord. There are women and men that don't know that they live in the Lord's house. If you don't walk with Christ, you won't know. I still have a car that protects me from the rain, cold, and heat. No weapon formed against me shall prosper and I shall refute every tongue that comes against me. I am an example. The Lord is my shepherd. Jesus is all I need. I cry and pout all the time, but the Lord waits on me with loving kindness. I have blessed others with money while I myself am homeless. I only had $300. I gave $100 away. He has me in His hands and I want to remember that whenever the enemy attacks me, I will look at what the Lord did for me. Peace is my portion for this season. This is to show myself and others that God is really all you need. Papa, I thank You for all Your work. All things work for the good of those who love You. I'm using the gym to shower. It gives me a reason to work out again consistently. Jesus is funny! He said you needed that consistent bath time too. Oh my gosh! That's so mean, but true.

Honestly, Jesus, You are funny LOL. My goodness, Jesus, keep on LOL. Anyway! I want to remember the joy of the Lord is my strength. The enemy tries to convince me that this is punishment, but there would be no peace if it was. There is no rest for the wicked. I'm so glad I know my Bible. Thank You, God. Thank You for teaching me the things I needed to know. I love You so. Even when things look kind of gloomy, I know You are still there. Here. You are here, in Jesus name, Amen.

24 April 2024

Wow! Wow. Wow. I thought it would be a disappointment to not write in the journal, as I'm finally reading it. God, You have done it all and is still doing it. The Lord Almighty is His name, the King of Kings. I am healed and I am still Yours. A year later, things didn't happen the way I originally thought, but reading through, regardless Your hand was over it. Wow. My God You are amazing. So much has changed and I am Your brand new creation made for You and only You. The promises still stand as I am writing from the promised land. Here we are Papa. You carried me through. Now your word has to perform in Jesus name. Amen.

Chapter 8

Strength In The Promised Land

Navigating life's journey alongside the Lord has often felt like an uphill battle for me. Time and again, I've found myself devising grand plans, only to hear His gentle yet firm voice whisper, "No, I need you to focus on this instead." It's a humbling realization that some pursuits serve merely as distractions, siphoning away precious time and energy that could be better spent in His service. In my quest to grasp all that God has in store for me, I am reminded of the importance of obedience to the divine path illuminated before me. It's true that the thought of adhering too closely can seem daunting; many may shy away from the pressure of maintaining such a dedicated walk. Yet I have come to understand that God's grace and mercy abound, easing the burdens that can accompany strict devotion. The nature of my relationship with Him thrives on this understanding, nurtured by my fervent prayer for Him to clear away all distractions from my path. I long for the fulfillment of the promises that await, and I realize that, for some, the prospect of delay seems to be merely an accepted part of their journey. Jesus himself has called us not to fret over tomorrow, reminding us that anxiety leads nowhere fruitful, and the sacred texts caution us about the deceptive inclinations of the human heart when it comes to our intentions and aspirations. With this wisdom in mind, I strive to remain steadfast, fixated on the divine trail ahead, trusting that every step taken in obedience draws me closer to the abundant life He has designed for me.

"All a person's ways seem pure to them, but motives are weighed by the Lord . Commit to the Lord whatever you do, and he will establish your plans."
Proverbs 16:2-3 NIV

"In their hearts humans plan their course, but the Lord establishes their steps."
Proverbs 16:9 NIV

I was promised the gift of marriage and a sanctuary to call my own—a home that, given my circumstances, felt almost like a distant dream. Yet, here I am, dear reader, writing these very words while grappling with the harsh reality of being physically homeless. My car, a cramped space meant only for travel, has become my solitary refuge. It's hard to reconcile the bright promise of faith with the darkness of my current situation. You see, we all desire to dwell in the warmth of goodness rather than endure the refining fires of hardship. There are still countless areas within me that need His gentle touch; I know I do not yet reflect His image as I should. The first night I closed my eyes in that car felt like an unbearable weight pressing down on my heart. Devastation coursed through me—crushed under the enormity of my circumstances, rendered nearly voiceless in my grief. Earlier that evening, at a church family dinner, I met a girl whose story mirrored my own in such an unsettling way it felt like God made the universe echo back to me. She, too, had come chasing after the promise of marriage, only to find herself in the cruel grip of uncertainty. Two weeks in Oklahoma had unfolded for her, devoid of job prospects, financial stability, or a place to truly belong. Unlike me, who had managed to escape each night to a hotel or a newfound friend's couch, she had been sleeping in her car since day one. It hit me like a jolt of electricity; the Lord was making it abundantly clear that I needed to make a decision that night I met her. As I mulled over our conversation, I felt the tug of desperation; I was bereft of funds and overtaken by the thought of spending another night in the car. Asking for help felt like the only viable option left, but the weight of pride held me back. I looked around —no one seemed to notice my silent call for aid, and a deep knowing settled in my heart: this was all part of His divine plan.

I kept my Bible open on Psalm 91 that night, feeling the weight of my worries wash over me as tears streamed down my cheeks. The Lord, in His infinite compassion, enveloped me in a peaceful slumber, allowing me to rest without interruption. In the stillness of the night, as I lay there cradled by His love, I felt the burdens of my distress begin to lift, the promise of His presence reassuring me deep within my soul. As dawn broke, I awoke with a renewed spirit and made my way to the gym, eager to meet up my new friend but even more determined to find solace in that space, even if it was primarily for a hot shower. I couldn't help but chuckle at the thought of just washing up, but I knew I'd sneak in a few workouts, too. After securing my membership, I marveled at how God orchestrated every detail of this new chapter. The price was certainly a stretch for my budget, reminding me of the wilderness that had once enslaved my thinking, chaining me to a mentality of scarcity. Yet, in His grace, God had set me free, and a bright, sweet-spirited girl at the front desk welcomed me with a smile, a divine nudge encouraging me to embrace all the gym had to offer. My spirit danced with joy; as I reconnected with my passion for fitness, I reflected on how far I had come. There was a time when I was a girl with a heart cloaked in deceit, yearning for validation from others, lost in the rhythm of superficial desires, enchanted by the lure of pagan melodies while losing weight for all the wrong reasons. But the Lord, in His marvelous wisdom, "flipped that thang!" Here I stood, a liberated spirit created anew, filled with purpose and passion.

After my gym session, I ventured to the park, where the sun filtered through the trees and the world felt alive. In that moment, God reminded me that even in the absence of a physical home, I was enveloped in His protection. My car—my humble shelter from the rain's cascade and the winds' fury—was a testament to His grace. While I may not have a roof of worldly structure over my head, His goodness and love pursued me relentlessly, ensuring that I dwell in His presence. My spirit thrived, knowing that my cup would overflow with blessings as He accompanied me through life's valleys and mountaintops. Fear had no dominion over me; with the Lord as my keeper, tyranny lay far from my reach, and terror would not draw near stated in Isaiah 54. I learned the beauty of contentment, understanding that the world, in all its complexities, is the Lord's domain. Despite what many might say, declaring it the devil's playground, we must remember—it's the Lord's devil. He cannot tread upon God's children without His divine permission. Wherever He calls me, I will go—whether it be to the gym for a cleansing shower or to the park for a leisurely stroll, every step belongs to Him. The laundromat where I wash my clothes—all part of His provision. Everything in this vast world is His creation, and He ensures avenues of protection and peace for His beloved children. Our Father holds the keys to it all; as His children, we possess the extraordinary privilege to approach His throne with boldness and confidence. A child in a loving home doesn't hesitate before rifling through the fridge in search of a snack; they know with unwavering faith that their parents will nourish them. In the same way, we are invited to reach into the abundance of our Father, fearing nothing as we claim our rightful place as His heirs with Christ Jesus. Praise God!

"For those who are led by the Spirit of God are the children of God. The Spirit you received does not make you slaves, so that you live in fear again; rather, the Spirit you received brought about your adoption to sonship. And by him we cry, " Abba, Father." The Spirit himself testifies with our spirit that we are God's children. Now if we are children, then we are heirs—heirs of God and co-heirs with Christ, if indeed we share in his sufferings in order that we may also share in his glory."

Romans 8:14-17 NIV

May 2024

It hurts so much because I still love differently than most. I learned how to skip stages in life because of certain traumas. There were so many times that I was in something traumatic and I tried to cloud my mind with fantasy to get out of it. It made me want to live life fast. To go after accomplishments for approval to show that I am worthy. God doesn't give goals, for His approval. He loves us, even when we don't do the big things. We can't earn His love. He loves in the slow seasons too. Just because I'm not doing something huge, doesn't mean He loves me less. He is still here in these moments. God is unchanging. I, too, should love even in the slow moments and have confidence in the fact that God is Holy, Just, and Unchanging. I should be changing for the better and will be. There will be slow seasons and I must enjoy every second of it to thrive as a child of God. Stability is going through the same things and not being moved. God has so much love, mercy, and grace that He did it for you at record speeds. Now, you must slow down because He is giving you promises and there will be other promises, but they will come at a slower pace. You must know that God still loves you and isn't upset that you are not accomplishing worldly things. He knows your parents specifically. Your dad would ask and tell you to push to get a job and good education. Show them how I have shown you. The only way to prosperity is with God; not with money or worldly wisdom. Your mother is always buying something new. She has so much already, while we are on the topic of contentment. My mother wants to get married. I trust and believe that she will because our Father is good to me and He has and will use me to catapult the family into His purpose. God said when I become prosperous, to not give money, but to show them how I became prosperous. God can't skip the season because He loves you so much.

Unlearn that. Unlearn those things that are not like Him. Accomplishments don't make you worthy of God's love. He already loves you. God sees you walking upright in a slow season. That does not mean punishment. He is still here and will always be. Create a routine. It will help you to continue speaking to him every morning. You don't have to switch up. Be able to adjust though. Pray and worship through mornings, but keep talking to Him throughout the day. God is going to prepare you in every season. Don't force the promises. When God gives you one, trust that he will do it again and He will give you instructions to you and your husband. You can't be rushing your husband. Slow down. Enjoy the new life God has given you. You have seen His hand and His works. God is with you and will surely be. Remember all that He took you out of. It is coming to a close. You will forget the shame of your youth, but won't be able to go this fast later. Learn to love the same. God is still blessing you. This promise isn't a reward, but He wants you to enjoy it because he knows you won't be able to if you go in like how you are now. Love the same view. Love the same things, so you will always appreciate them. God knew me before I was in my mother's womb. He made me a certain way. God created me as a helpmate. I want to be provided for. I don't want hard labor. I want to help in labor and still work but not for money. I don't like money. I believe Papa doesn't like it either. He gives it because we can't do anything without it. Don't worry about the debts, God is going to pay them off. I don't know how, but the devil wants me to think that I need to handle it. God took everything out of my hands. God paid it all. Those debts were when you weren't walking with him. He has taken it over now. Amber, you wanted to be provided for and God has done it. He kept you with food and a roof, a place to shower, and a place of scenery. Don't take it for granted.

You have a kingdom friend with you in this season of homelessness. Don't take it for granted. God is using her and she will need you next. Learn to love the same. God will not let you miss anything that is for you. The same is good. Our God is the same yesterday, today and forevermore. It's a good thing to be the same. God will do the changing, not you. It's okay to slow down. Don't live life in haste. You are at a point and have not gone backward because of Jesus. He loves you very much. It's okay to love the same natural hair too. God will give you long natural hair, if it's in His will. You must know that you are loved with whatever! Natural is the best. Your husband loves natural hair. Do not be afraid. God has so much for you. He wants you to be the happy real you. You don't have to fake it. God is removing the Egypt inside of you now. Your vulnerability is what helps the kingdom. God loves you so much. You can breathe. Worship and praise is your weapon. Prayer is important too. Continue doing the things of God. He trusts you. You must not hold your breath, but embrace every situation. You've learned to be content. Be that. You are not lazy. God made you a certain way. Go back to God's original design. He wants you as his original design. You are enough. Don't listen to the serpent, Eve. You are enough. Eat from every other tree, except this one. Don't cross the line that God didn't design for you. It will cause death to your fruit and your spirit. Sin pulls you away from God. The fear of God is respect. You don't want to be away from Him. He is just. Jesus can redeem you but you don't want to keep putting Him on the cross in vain. Our God is so beautiful in all His ways. I love You, God. All of You. I love You, Papa. I love You, Jesus. I love You, Holy Spirit. Thank You for being my comforter, counselor, and all other things. This life would be nothing without You. Thank You for choosing me. God, I couldn't do it without You. Be secure in your royalty with God. David, you are the anointed king. Saul wasn't ready and couldn't handle the promise because of his false humility. He was insecure and eventually thought he could do what God told him not to, but you, David. Here is your double anointing. God loves you.

Chapter 9

Recompense And Restoration

There was a dream I had many moons ago, a vivid tableau of frozen moments that played across my mind like a haunting melody. I was on a school bus, surrounded by faces I recognized—their innocence reminded me of the vibrancy of childhood. We were young children, maybe too young to comprehend the gravity of our situation. As the bus slowly descended, the water enveloped us like a thick, all-consuming blanket, transforming a mundane ride into a surreal game, an unnerving test handed down by some unseen force. I was the only one gripped by panic, desperately scanning the faces around me, hoping to spark some flicker of realization in the others, but they remained entranced, staring into a void that seemed to swallow their very souls. Once the entire bus was submerged, their apathy was suffocating. I was left alone in my terror, a lone warrior in a sea of oblivion, pleading with their silence—a silence so profound it echoed in my heart. It struck me then that my mission was clear: I must help those who are drowning without awareness.

The world is rife with currents of overwhelming emotion, pain, and the suffocating weight of evil that drags us under. God had implored us to live life more abundantly. Why would we rush back to Him when He bestows upon us this precious gift of existence? Why do we let ourselves drown, even as He provides the map to liberation? The promised land is more than a mere geographic destination; it's an intricate cloth embroidered with threads of emotion, mental clarity, and spiritual awakening. In a luminous dream, Jesus spoke to me with weight and tenderness, saying, "When you receive the person you love, remember that you deserve to live." In that sacred moment, He gifted me a double portion—blessings unearned, bestowed upon me purely from His boundless grace.

Among the cherished gifts I received from Jesus in my dream was a delightful and whimsical keychain, with the image of a beloved childhood character: Thomas the Tank Engine. He is a cheeky, spirited little locomotive, full of life and wonder. With a personality that often straddles the line between playful enthusiasm and a tendency to be a bit fussy, he has a knack for finding himself in amusing predicaments. Thomas, in his relentless excitement, frequently attempts tasks that would be wiser left to the larger, more seasoned engines of the railway. Yet, despite the occasional mishap, dark clouds of trouble never linger long in Thomas' world. He shakes off his troubles with a determined puff of steam and soon finds himself bustling with renewed vigor, dutifully playing his role in the bustling yard and pridefully managing his own branch line, a slice of the railway that fills him with immense pride and joy! As for the second gift, it eludes my memory with frustrating elusiveness, though I believe they were keys that accompanied the heartwarming keychain. Keys to a much grander kingdom, the Kingdom of God. They felt like a tangible promise. It was as if Jesus deemed me worthy to hold them, inviting me into a realm where hope and grace reign supreme. In that moment, with the weight of those keys in my hand, I felt a stirring in my spirit—a connection to something greater than myself, a journey that was just beginning to unfold.

For me, this promised land embodies healing, the transformative power of becoming the person I was destined to be for Him. I now release worries about the promises laid before me. If He proclaimed it, His word is law. Time and time again, I have witnessed His miracles throughout my journey with Him. God alone knows the blueprints He has meticulously crafted for our lives, guiding the steps of the righteous with unwavering certainty. When He called me to return to South Carolina from Oklahoma, confusion washed over me like a relentless tide, and frustration simmered just beneath the surface. I believed I had arrived in my promised land, yet faith is a journey of trust. After seeking confirmation and receiving the provisions necessary to make that transition, He unveiled to me the marvels of restoration and recompense. There was a deep-seated renewal within me, a rebirth that allowed me to appreciate the wonders of life that surrounded me at home—the smiles of loved ones, the gentle rustle of the trees, the laughter echoing in the air. In the wilderness, I found humility, even within what I had perceived as my true promised land, learning the importance of patience and faith. And through it all, God has transformed me into a vessel to uplift others, to guide them toward their own light amid the shadows.

The LORD has made proclamation to the ends of the earth: "Say to Daughter Zion, 'See, your Savior comes! See, his reward is with him, and his recompense accompanies him.' " They will be called the Holy People, the Redeemed of the LORD; and you will be called Sought After, the City No Longer Deserted.
Isaiah 62:11-12 NIV

17 September 2024

Papa, I love You. Thank You for always keeping me updated. "Pray before you let them in your life." My breakthrough is nigh. I'm excited! I'm so happy. Nothing has really happened other than God pulling me out of the pit once again last night. Good things did happen today and my heart is so full. My home is growing and getting closer. My husband is beginning his business. Oh Papa, please keep him on Your path and grow his business for him to have family time and be present as a father too. Grow our love and family quickly. Abba, bring him out of Egypt into a promised land You swore to give his ancestors. Show him Your love. Remind him that he is the richest because he has God on his side. You walk with him and yet he doesn't fully understand it. Papa, I pray that my sight is restored fully to what you have and purpose for me. As a woman, I am to help grow and multiply. My husband gives me seed while I take his seed and grow it into something of a miracle. Of course, I couldn't do any of it without God's hand, but with His blessing and because He said it, I can. A little girl walked over to me while crying. She was so sweet; her little self. Curious and looking around. My heart was so happy to have a baby in my arms. To have many children is a blessing. It's like your very own army. An army for God! I can't wait, Papa. I know it's not easy caring for so many children, but with You anything is possible. You make what would be difficult to most, easy for those who were called to do it and You watch over and give us grace to do it. Father, please grace me to be a homemaker, a mother of many. I can't ask for grace alone, without asking for the grace of provision for my husband. Rest and set the grace of love for his family and beasts on his heart. So many men struggle to provide for one, even three, children. You know how many children and blessings we will have therefore I pray for Your covering over us as we are elevated. Provide for our every need and remind us that if You bring us into a higher responsibility, You too, will make provision when the time comes. Thank You, Father, for our blessing. Thank You for gracing James with a Kingdom Business. Coming from selling drugs so selling technology. There were two sales in just about an hour and I know it was You. Bring the people to his business. I made these prayers for myself when I thought I would start a business, but not now. I know the vision I received. My passion is to feed people and children. When the time comes, God will provide it for me. Right now, I'm in purpose through healing and loving those placed around me. I prayed that God would bring the people to me and lead them to buy my products. I now transfer that prayer to my husband, not for himself, but to provide for his growing family to provide seed. I pray that James continues to plant good seeds among the people and give glory to God in all his ways. I am the person that loves God and I have partially accepted that my relationship with God is different than my husband's relationship. So Father, I pray that he hears You clearly as You grow him suddenly in this hour, open his heart and mind, and grace him with Your beautiful glory. Let him praise you every time he thinks of what You did in his life, open his heart and open his mind. If I am the reminder that is supposed to speak to him. Please help me heal and open my mouth. Bless us always. Thank You for blessing him. Thank You for loving him by watching after his home. Bring love, peace, and sobriety completely. Take away the alcoholic tastes, Papa. Don't let him miss it. Destroy that glutton spirit in Jesus' name. May he put to rest the old him while loving the new him. The version of him, God, that You chose to heal and love on in Jesus' name. Amen. Papa, thank You for my husband. I pray that he fully embraces the heart You give him before we come together. Thank You for teaching me patience and love. I love You.

I am so grateful for my husband that God has given me. I will no longer focus on the event, but just know that God has already given me a husband that loves me. God loves me so much. I will not allow the enemy to make me focus on anything other than God and His love for me; That He has put in a man. Papa told me many blessings would come as long as I am not focused on other things. I could miss the things that seem small, but are actually big things. Releasing expectations of people makes room for so much more. I love my time with James. I miss him when he is away. I'm also going to miss our alone time. I love to be around him. When we are together, I know You are always watching and covering us. My heart swells at the thought of him. I won't focus on him and his actions, but on what God said. Eventually it will come to pass and I don't have to chase him. Let him come to me. He will initiate and my heart will fill to the brim that day. Papa, I will keep praying for him. I love him and I want the best for him. I pray for his health and sleep that You release good health and sleep over him tonight. He works so hard and I don't want him to learn the hard way of resting. Teach him that he will enjoy not having to work all the time. He has a partner. Not only that, but that You cover the things he doesn't see. Papa, bless him with abundance and all of Your good things. You have many and I ask that he is blessed and first covered with the blood of Jesus and forgiven of his and his family's past sins. Papa, bless him abundantly with wisdom, knowledge, prosperity, light, selflessness, generosity, joy, open eyes, bold fire of the Holy spirit in Jesus name. That's what I want to pray for! The fire of the Holy Spirit to move in his life. Take over his tongue and use him to plant and sow. Papa, pour the fire of the Holy Spirit on his soul encamp around him and make home with him. Love on him. Father, I don't expect his fire to be like mine, but I pray for You to pour Your leadership over him. I know he was made to lead Your people. May You teach him Your holy word and may he remember how rich he is because he has You. Papa, love him back whole and be his everlasting Rock. Every demon that comes against him will be shamed by the blood of Jesus and no weapon shall prosper. Papa, I love to pray for him. You put the need to talk about him so I could talk about him to You! I will. LOL! Papa, Your son has been doing so good lately! I know it is You! Papa, can he stricken up on his sobriety? I know this isn't build-a-man, but I will always pray for my husband's sobriety. He should be sober while leading always. Leave wine and beer for those who are perishing. In the mighty name of Jesus, James is not perishing, but living! I bind up alcohol experiences and ties in him and his bloodline in the name of Jesus and every chain is broken. It is broken. I loose and release him in sobriety by the blood of the Lamb, amen! Papa, I pray that he tries to wean his puppy from his bedroom now in the name of Jesus. Papa, this one is a harder prayer LOL. Papa, all beasts of the field worship and obey You. Papa, can You go to James' dog and tell him it's time to grow up? LOL. I know You can, I just mean it as a request lol. I'm grateful for You always. I understand that James needs to do better in training him, so I pray for that. A dog can't lay in our bed together. I mean it can, but no. Not in our marriage bed. Maybe I'm the crazy one, but I don't want the dog in our bed together as we sleep. He will want to be there when it's our intimate time too. Then he will be whining. While we are trying to have our time together. I don't want that. I suppose it's going to be like that with our children as well. Hmm. Well, papa, I'm going to need help with that already LOL. I guess the babies can be put to sleep, but an animal though? Okay! I need help. Papa, that's his dog. I'm not that big on dogs, but I love all living cute things. Mostly. I mean it's fine as long as it doesn't whine when outside the bedroom. That's all I ask. I pray that I'm able to stand on that. We don't have to get rid of the dog, just shouldn't be taken care of like a human. Or better yet, better care of than a human. Papa, You would agree a dog is not as important as a human. I agree with You. Papa, can James have that knowledge? LOL. Okay! I will stop because You're going to get on me LOL. Next thing is, Your son puts a lot of pressure on himself to be the best. Ease his mind that he has already won with You. I don't know what it is like to be a man or what the thoughts of a man are. So You know that I'm not trying to figure it out. Sometimes I think the competitive mindset can go too far. Show him that he doesn't need to push himself to be the best for man's approval, when he already has God's approval. Save him from corporate chains and work traps. Release him from the chains of being a workaholic. Bring peace and love to Your son. Protect him from witches and warlocks trying to take the glory from You. Destroy their high altars and smash their idols to pieces. Bring about to James, a new foundation of precious stones. Papa, I love Your son so much. I want to tell him so bad. I want to tell him so bad. I should tell him. I don't need to hear it back. I just want him to know it. He is my everything that I prayed for. He isn't completed, but the fact that Papa is working on him, I know he is what I prayed for. I don't need the title to tell him that I love him. I just do. Whenever I have the opportunity, I hope that I can. The God opportunity and nothing else. When God allows me to, I won't be in a panic. I don't care about who should say it first. That's stupid. I want him to know it and I don't need anything back. I love him because he is worthy of love by being himself. Not what he provides for me, not by his title, or what he does. This way he will know when my title does change, nothing else will. It was given by God and nobody could take it away. Thank You, Papa. Thank You for an honorable man. A man that I was made for. A man that I don't mind giving my heart to. I was made for him out of his rib. My heart was made for the man. I'm so grateful. Papa, brought me to my husband. To my dear husband, I love you and I thank God for you. I love who you are. You cover me and protect me before I was even fully yours. You watched and learned about me. You favored me and my heart. I appreciate everything you do for me because you don't have to, but you want to. A noble man you are. I'm so happy that God made me for you. I love you, husband and Jesus does too.

19 September 2024

Abba, good morning! I love You. How are You this morning? Your glory is always surrounding us. My body is tired, but my soul is energized! LOL. Papa, how are You really? I know You're always good, but what are Your thoughts right now? I know great disappointment for the country. Papa, I definitely understand why You're disappointed in us. Papa, bless us please. those that walk in Your righteous way. Don't destroy us. It is still a blessing to live in America. The great Babylon is and will fall. You have prophesied that thousands of years ago. The great Babylon. Papa, did You really want me to move out of America? Where will I go? I know I shouldn't wait around for my husband, but You taught me patience and to wait for those to turn back. I have Your love inside of me. I know not to run back for everyone, but I don't want to leave my one flesh behind to suffer judgment. If I am here, please don't bring judgment on the land. Please Papa. You said if there are even 10 people, You won't destroy us. There were false people telling me that I'm going to get judgment too by being there or here, but I know You have a way of doing things. Papa, please don't think of this as disobedience. I'm wanting good for America. I know there are nasty people, wicked people, but let's turn as many back to You and then we will move. Father, whoever wins the election, protect Your righteous ones. Place Your spirit in us and may we guide people to You in love and truth. Papa, I do love America. I do. I don't want to move anywhere. I want to visit places, but not move. You have given me many visions that I cannot fulfill on my own, so I know they are things You've given me. Papa, You told me that I would have a business to help feed and shelter people. If it's here then I am happy. I don't have to move out of state. It's always the feeling of being away from my family that I believe was pushing me the most. To get away from the old me. The old me is gone now though. I'm cleaned with a pure heart and when I'm married, my family doesn't go with me. A gift! My husband clings to me! A gift! Marriage is a gift! I have the greatest gift of all time. God orchestrated mine. We have agape love and I'm so happy. My family doesn't go with me. I know my joy isn't in another location but my joy is here and from within. I had such a good day yesterday building and helping my husband at work. Working on the coolers! LOL. I knew it was You! Normally, I'm mad at doing things like that, but I loved it. Helping him and achieving something. It looks so nice and Papa, you made him so smart! His foresight is so good. He has valuable opinions. He didn't just take advice from my other coworker. Lol. I didn't think about it but it's good. When things do fail though, I don't want to put him down. He is so so smart. I don't want him to think he's not good enough or dumb. He really is a good man at heart, but there are also a lot of bad seeds that show and have grown. They need to be cut down. Papa, I know every prayer was heard. He will step into sobriety. He will be saved and he will be baptized. My Lord, teach him Your decrees and laws. His eyes will be opened at baptism, I believe it. In Jesus name, I pray for his repentant heart. Lord, You are close to him in this hour. Please show him Your way. Papa, You also showed me a house months ago. The house. I'm still believing for it. I will probably forget about it, but I know it will happen. When I was talking with James about it before I left, I said to him, "give me a year." Maybe that was you speaking and maybe it was not. Either way, the Lord, You will carry me through. I know it's mine and every demon, devil, placeholder, and counterfeit must flee in Jesus name! I plead the blood over every single thing that is mine in the promised land. I'm here now, so demons must go in the mighty name of Jesus Christ. Thank You, Papa. It's all You and Your servants. May I continue to find everlasting favor in Your eyes. I love You so. Amen.

Epilogue

We may not always fully comprehend the twists and turns of life, but each step we take in alignment with God's divine guidance brings us closer to our ultimate good. As it is beautifully expressed in the scriptures, particularly Romans 8:28, "And we know that in all things God works for the good of those who love him, who have been called according to his purpose." This reassurance is like a gentle echo in our hearts, reminding us that while trials may come our way, God's hand is always orchestrating our path for His glory and our good. Throughout my journey, I have witnessed the transformative power of the Lord. The enemy, with his dark whispers, sought to belittle me by branding me as being terrible at English literature, lazy, and a homewrecker, attempting to sow seeds of doubt in my heart. Yet, amidst the turbulence, God spoke life and purpose over my being. He transformed my identity, gifting me the name "homemaker," a title that embodies love, care, and nurturing. He transformed my existence into that of an author, tasked with proclaiming His gospel and illuminating to the world that He remains dedicated to crafting individuals from the shadows of obscurity into the brilliance of significance.

This is no mere alteration of words, but a profound shift to show me my worth in His eyes. Indeed, the Lord is both faithful and wonderful, a steadfast companion through trials. He has mended my heart and healed my land, setting me free because I choose to walk in obedience to His perfect will. In a world endlessly searching for the elusive secret to life, we as believers stand firm in the knowledge that our true answer lies in a relationship with God Almighty, the Lord Christ Jesus, and the Holy Spirit. They are not hidden away; rather, they are the brilliant light illuminating our paths. To God be the glory now and forevermore. Amen and Amen.

Papa, You have been my unwavering foundation, tirelessly working to rebuild my life with lapis lazuli and the finest precious stones. That early morning, when the sun first kissed the horizon, You spoke the words of Isaiah 54 over me, wrapping them around my heart like a protective shield. Your promises are a melody that echoes in my soul, a testament to your faithfulness, and I hold onto the certainty that You will fulfill every single one of those sacred words You delivered. In the quiet moments of my day, I feel the strength of Your love, the reassurance that no matter the storms that may come, I am anchored in this divine truth. Your words resonate like a beautiful symphony, a promise that my life is being shaped into something magnificent and profound. As I sit here editing this book, I am filled with a flood of emotions, remembering the dream on September 20, 2016. It was then that you gifted me a vivid dream of giving birth. That dream was not merely a fleeting vision; it signified the birth and creation of this book and my journey towards You. Your surprises never cease to leave me in awe. I am deeply grateful. Thank You.

www.ingramcontent.com/pod-product-compliance
Lightning Source LLC
LaVergne TN
LVHW010452160826
845677LV00012B/2457

* 9 7 9 8 8 9 5 6 9 4 2 9 9 *